GOD KNOWS

GOD KNOWS

It's Not About Us

If you want More

You Better Die

This Is All There Is

Here

BLAYNEY COLMORE

To order additional copies of this book, contact:
Xlibris Corporation
1-888-795-4274
www.Xlibris.com
Orders@Xlibris.com
28573

CONTENTS

An Odyssey of OH Home & Home 11

To The Reader, My Shrink 13

Red Alerts & Reality 16

Zone Notes 20

A Work Of Fancy 22

Our Hero 23

Boredom, Terror & Conversation 25

Entry Point Our Hero's Technicolor Self-discovery 28

Whales Making More Whales 30

Our Hero's Apparatus 44

Building Bigger Barns 53

OH Revisits His First Kiss Revealing The Origin of
     His Fear Of God 57

All's Fair in Love & War . . . And In A Herd 62

Seahorses 65

Pain And Inner Knowledge 77

Pipeline to God and Prayer A Religious Experience 79

Stigmata 83

Organized Religion as Self-Diddling 88

The Leather Bar A Study in Shame & Grace 89

Gertrude; Shame & Grace II 95

Good/Bad . . . Right/Wrong Reality Cannot Be Crippled 98

The Diving Dentist and The Olympic Sailor Dying On Holiday 102

Grunion Run In The Earth's Ether 107

Seeing Spots 109

Anson's Cheatin' Heart 113

The Old Randy Writer 121

The Atomic/Cellular Theory 125

OH Goes to Ground Zero 132

Red Tag Special 136

The Last Temptation of OH The F Word 139

OH Makes A Run For It 144

Epilogue 163

To my muse
You know who you are
even if I sometimes
forget.

Thanks to my wife Lacey who finds my writing somewhere between offensive and incomprehensible. More than any other person or piece of my life she makes it possible for me to do it.

And to Hugh Davies, Director of the Museum of Contemporary Art, San Diego, who bravely named me Writer-In-Residence a few years ago and, despite my weird vision, hasn't rescinded my title. Every day when I walk through the museum to my carrel in the museum library, I am moved by the daring vision of Hugh and his staff. Virginia Abblitt and Andee Hale, the two library directors during my tenure, have shown me uncommon hospitality.

I will not publicly embarrass my small circle of friends who will listen to me carry on about these matters that others think I should be locked up for. You, too, know who you are.

My sisters, one an editor, the other an administrative assistant in a legal aid office, appalled as they sometimes are by my lack of literary discipline, have behaved as if they think this effort is wonderful. And they have contributed their writing wisdom and discipline to make this a better book.

I would be remiss if I failed to mention Son, clockmaker without parallel, who provides a marker by which I get my bearings. Son came to America as a boat-person following the Viet Nam War. He apprenticed under a German clockmaker and now runs his own shop. He has been working on my French repeater, a 19th century carriage clock, for over four years. He has repaired it over and over only to see it rupture internally because of old, delicate parts that have been jimmied by previous incompetents. But he refuses to give up. Twice in the four years he has traveled to Switzerland to improve his skills.

Once a week I stop by his shop on my way to the museum. He and I pronounce curses on those who have worked previously on this clock. I worry that if he should ever succeed in making the clock run properly, and my weekly visits cease, my life would go off course like a ship that missed a critical mark.

An Odyssey of OH
Home & Home

Preface

Reality/God rules.
And there is that leviathan . . . Psalm 104:26

God Knows

God knows
I suppose
how our shadow slyly (or is it shyly?)
shows
what we'd hoped to
pose
as,

and how instead
God faces down
our fears   for us
and shows our shadow to
the seeker
from whom we
fled,

and the prey we have
prayed
we'd remain is instead
ambushed
locked in the
ravishing embrace we knew all along would do us
in.

To The Reader, My Shrink

Wondering

We will wonder for a
lifetime
what we were to make of this
lifetime
longing all the while for some sure
sign.

But the sign of Jonah
will be our only sign for this
lifetime
so
we will never know for certain in this
lifetime
whether wondering was worthwhile
or
was it all the while always just
fine?

From what source, one might wonder, would anyone gain the energy to write a book? Or the narcissism to think anyone would want to read it?

It beats therapy.

Here's what I would take to the therapist today; I can only imagine what these matters might look like by the time you read this. I am writing in the spring of 2005.

My friend, now my doctor, was a classmate in high school. And his wife was then his girlfriend. That was in Newport, Rhode Island in 1956. He and I were 16; his girlfriend was 17. We kept in sporadic but significant touch over the next 30 years until I moved to San Diego where he had lived since completing his internship. One attempt to renew the intensity our friendship had when we were teenagers aborted. Each of us was distracted, immersed in our professional lives, still hoping to find salvation there.

A few years later, as I was emerging from 30 years as parish pastor, moving toward reclusive writer, we met again and bonded, he and his wife, with my wife and me, fiercely. Maybe because we had acknowledged that life does not last forever.

Last week his wife was diagnosed with an aggressive form of leukemia. Less than two weeks ago she was on the golf course; today she is in the isolation unit in the hospital. Her immune system is being dismantled in hopes that she might rebuild her bone marrow with orderly cells that do not run riot.

The night before she went to the hospital, her husband, my longest-standing friend, asked her if she was terrified.

"No," she answered convincingly, "resolute. I was terrified watching my parents go through this, but doing it myself is not scary."

So, therapist/reader, could we talk about that? About how it is one calmly faces the inevitable dismantling of these cells? Is she a person of great faith? Not in any conventional sense. Not a church-goer. Not a reciter of creeds. But a woman grounded in reality. And that is what I am sponsoring as faith. The willingness and ability to embrace reality. I don't believe it is a skill available to young people, though young people can spot it in older people.

So let's push on to some evidence that our culture does not sponsor such a skill. In fact when the possibility of our end shows itself, our culture sends up a yellow, then orange, and finally red alert. "Stay away."

This volume of fiction is bent toward embracing reality, particularly those pieces of reality to which our culture attaches warning labels. It is not a "How To" book, though I would not be above writing one if I knew how to. It is, I hope, filled with pointers toward what sustains, and can delight us, in the season we have been given. And I hope it is fun.

This is an odyssey, Our Hero's odyssey as he wanders, sometimes seemingly without direction or purpose, toward the assured focusing of his quest. But before meeting OH, here's a sample of the obstacles our culture places between us and the ecstasy we are warned not to trust.

*   *   *

RED ALERTS & REALITY

President Bush has rushed back to Washington, interrupting his playtime at his Texas ranch, to sign a bill sending the matter of Teri Schiavo's feeding tube to a federal judge. In case today's headline has faded into obscurity, she was the woman in Florida who suffered irreversible brain damage during a heart attack and has been, for the past 15 years, sustained by a feeding tube in what we elegantly describe as a "persistent vegetative state". Her husband says she told him once that she would not wish to live like that and he petitioned to have the feeding tube removed.

Her parents, her sister and her brother believe she might recover and that her husband wants her dead for his own convenience. Likely there is plenty of family history in that mess, history written long before her heart attack.

So, a hard dilemma. How to resolve it? In our country the way we have agreed, when people reach an impasse, is to ask the courts to decide. Seems sad for a family to turn to the courts, but perhaps you know from your own family that we sometimes cannot agree. A courtroom beats homicide.

And so her family litigated. Over several years, at countless cost, Teri's husband's lawyers and her parents' lawyers argued their opposing views before judges. Finally, after many appeals and publicity, a brave judge in Florida ruled that her husband was the best person to know what she would have wanted, and that the best medical opinion was that she was unaware of her situation and unlikely to improve.

He gave permission for the feeding tube to be removed. Several higher courts, including the Supreme Court, affirmed his decision.

So finally the judge set a date certain for the feeding tube to be removed.

The Republican Congress passed and President signed, precedent—defying, legislation requiring the case to be heard in federal rather than Florida State Court. Unprecedented, because under our Constitution the legislature cannot intervene in matters before the court.

So why did they do this? Motives are nearly impossible to unravel, even our own. But it is fair to say that, whether cynical or not, the politicians were responding to what they perceived as a red alert. Danger!

In order to make sense of this, and perhaps to understand why I am writing this book, sending OH on a journey with an indisputable outcome, I list a few other matters on the public agenda.

A 31 year old man had a fatal heart attack while skiing at Mammoth Mountain in California recently. He was a graduate of The University of San Diego, a Jesuit Universit under the authority of the Roman Catholic bishop of San Diego. The dead man's family asked that his funeral be in the University chapel. The man had run a couple of nightclubs, apparently raw and wild places. One of them had a largely gay clientele on Saturday nights. No doubt there is more to it, but that's what we have been given in the news.

The Roman Catholic bishop of San Diego refused to permit his funeral to be held at USD, or in any other parish in the San Diego Diocese. They said his business did not conform to the moral teachings of the Church.

This man's funeral was held in St. Paul's Episcopal Cathedral, which for some years has been a gathering place for Integrity, an organization for gay Episcopalians and their friends.

The bishop was responding to what he perceived as a red alert. Danger!

The Roman Catholic Church has warned the faithful against reading Dan Brown's sensational best seller, **The Da Vinci Code**, which, among other fictional devices, portrays Jesus and Mary Magdalene as having been married. Red Alert there, all right.

The recently appointed Director of the CIA, Porter Goss, in an appearance before a Congressional committee, solemnly listed the countless ways in which the United States remains dangerously vulnerable to another terrorist attack. This one, he warns, likely more devastating than the Twin Towers attack. He promised not to jerk us around with changing the alert colors, but he said he would not leave us needlessly vulnerable. Perhaps just leave it at red?

Several Imax movie theaters in the southern United States have refused to show a film about undersea volcanoes, not because there is violence or sex to offend, but because the scientists in the film suggest that the volcanoes may be older than biblical fundamentalists believe the world to be.

President Bush has named to head the World Bank (does it seem at all paradoxical to you that the President of the United States appoints the Head of the World Bank?) Paul Wolfowitz, a man associated in the international community with pressing for our invasion of Iraq against the weight of world opinion.

And John Bolton, who is on public record as saying there is no such thing as the United Nations, and that the United States should never be bound by its decisions, has been nominated to be our ambassador to that body.

Yesterday (March 20, 2005) Condoleeza Rice, American Secretary of State, arranged her schedule on her Asian trip so that she could attend Palm Sunday services in a Protestant Church in China and use the occasion to jab China in the matter of freedom of worship.

Donald Rumsfeld, the Secretary of Defense (Offense?), when asked to defend the small size of the troop deployment to Iraq, a matter now famously attributed to his determination to downsize our Army for such operations, yesterday told reporters that Turkey was to blame. Because Turkey's refusal to permit their country to be a staging area for our troops meant we had too few troops to capture or kill the insurgents who have been wreaking havoc ever since. Blame the foreigner.

A random selection of evidence that our culture has taught us to be reality averse. When faced with reality that does not conform to what we expect or want, we revert to fancy.

All that, along with my sadness that my wife hates the sandals I bought, ones with the spring coil support, so much, she refuses to walk with me when I wear them, are some of the matters I would be taking before my therapist if I were not spewing them out to you, dear reader, who will have paid me rather than my paying the therapist.

So you can see where the energy and motivation for writing a book come from.

Thank you.

I hope OH and I do not take out on you our frustration in knowing we will never again in our lifetime (I am 65) see the stock market climb back to the insane heights it did during the nifty 90s. How many of you would take Bill Clinton back, libido and all?

A journalist friend told me that he interviewed protesters at a Bush-For-President rally. He asked them who they would like instead. They all said Bill Clinton. How many of us would admit that publicly?

And that is what this book is arranged around. Whether we can afford, ever, to let the lusty energy in us see light. Or must we keep it tightly wrapped, surrendering the power to run things to those who pose as guardians of our morality and safety? Even at the expense of what we know in our loins is real. Must we forever mistrust and betray our longings? A design for emotional fascism.

In a recent interview Joe Biden, the sensible, even sometimes fun Senator from Delaware, deplored John Kerry's having let anything except the fight against terrorism gain focus during his run for President. Biden said he is certain that if you line up the economy, retirement income, medical care, civil liberties, tax rates, education, child care, and tell the American people we must give it all up to be protected against terrorism, we would no doubt all jump at that Faustian bargain.

If he is right Osama Bin Laden has won.

If he is wrong, and I am betting that he is, then this pendulum is going to swing the other way. Consider this book a move to give hope to people who want to keep their sense of humor supple. OH, hero of this odyssey, will work to keep alive your appetite for justice, your excitement and belief that we can afford for our life to be about something more than merely seeking safety. And that the task of a holy life is to keep alive the sense of wonder, the conviction that it is impossible to fit our lives into any neat scheme or creed. Reality trumps creeds. One day, soon I hope, we will regain the adventuresome agenda that has been bullied underground.

Faith is a bet that you can live your life as if it matters, even though you'll never be able to collect on the bet. It's a good bet. It is Pascal's wager.

Zone Notes

For some years I have sent out through email a piece of writing called Notes From Zone 4 (from Vermont where we spend the gentle months), and Notes From Zone 10 (San Diego, where we retreat from Vermont winter). They seem to go out about once a week, run a couple of pages long and focus on matters too varied to fit into some scheme. You can receive the Zone Notes by writing me at blayneyc@earthlink.net.

They are meant to appeal to those parts in us that are hungry for adventure, the parts that spill over the boundaries, that dare us to embrace reality. Even when reality disappoints or overturns our hopes.

Dick Trelease, my mentor, whom I buried recently, said anyone who thinks that God doesn't have a sense of humor has never considered how we humans reproduce. (He said this before the explosion of reproductive techniques recently developed, but none that I have yet heard described negates his insight.) You will see references, subtle and not so subtle, to this wise insight throughout this odyssey.

And finally, religion, that confounds so much of the world, especially the way we Americans practice it. Though I understand, and have contributed to the wish to fit human belief into some scheme we can all salute, as I grow closer to the dissolution of the arrangement of cells that has been identified as Blayney Colmore for nearing seven decades, I have become clear that we cannot conceive such a scheme. And need not.

After 40 years as an ordained priest I am still surprised when people suggest I am closer to God or have more direct access to spiritual depth than they do. But then I still can't quite bear the reality that my stock broker doesn't know what the market is going to do today. Or that my doctor is playing the odds because no one really knows what's happening inside my skin, or why.

Ancient and modern wisdom provide insights into the nature of reality. But that's it. Insights, not conclusions. Physicists have acknowledged that. We dreamers need to do the same.

And understand it as good news. These open-ended, unlimited possibilities.

Write me at *blayneyc@earthlink.net* and we'll explore together. In the meantime, wander through this book in the spirit in which I wrote it, with an inquiring and, give yourself some deserved credit, discerning mind.

I also have a blog, www.blayneyblog.blogspot.com where I provoke most days.

A Work Of Fancy

What follows is a work of fiction. If you think you have found yourself, or me, in the narrative, doubt it. And don't bother to call your lawyer. If you feel confused by the direct address of author to reader, be assured it is OH speaking to you. Sometimes OH channels through the author. The author has surrendered all claims to ownership of what follows. It is natural enough to want to identify which pieces of a narrative may have come from the author's experience. The author has followed OH into places he never has, nor ever would dare to go himself. Perhaps you will dare to follow also. Perhaps not. I hope you will. OH, I suspect, having surrendered all normal prerogatives, is beyond caring. It is your choice.

You have in your hands an odyssey, a tale of wonder and adventure. Sex and death. **The New York Times** insists that an odyssey must begin and end in the same place. Since, as quantum physics has shown, the seeming space between any two phenomena is illusion, every story is an odyssey. The alpha is the omega. What we have captured, in word or picture, is illusion. If the story works, the reader/hearer will recognize not only herself, but the place from which the hero comes and the place to which the hero goes.

OUR HERO

The hero of this story will be called "Our Hero," OH, because he is. He is living his life as we imagine we might have lived ours. Wondering with his every breath. As, in fact, we are living ours. Though we are loathe to claim it. And our conscious mind insists it's not so. He stands in the stead of the ego, giving ego a much needed rest, a holiday it has earned but rarely been granted in the recent history of the anxious western world. OH is not Everyman, but a particular portion of Everyman, that portion we might have once called Ego. Or self. Not exactly self-consciousness, but unrelenting consciousness of himself. OH stands in for us, making his way through his life in a manner that implicates us, leaving us holding the bag of our own choices. Conscious and unconscious. Sometimes the narrator, who chooses mostly to remain in the wings, will jump in and describe the hero's actions, chiefly to relieve you, dear reader, of boredom and terror, the twin emotions that are inescapable for those of us who have chosen existence in the flesh. That relief, while you may regard it as letting us off the hook too easily, is offered in hopes that you will stay tuned when things get dicey. You can watch it like a foreign movie. Interesting, fun, but nothing personal.

A word about ego, OH and identity. In ordinary speech ego has often come to mean conceited. Here it means something more like distinct identity. Yep, that's me. We seem to have elevated a factoid, that no two sets of fingerprints are identical, to a central place, as if this was what creation has been struggling to achieve. Uniqueness. Individuality. It is this exaggeration that has given ego a bad name. Ego, like virtually everything else around you—the moon, your computer, your mother, money, human coupling—is what the Shakers call a "gift for a season." It is simply given. We didn't earn it by our cleverness or hard work. Torture

23

ourselves as we do, we have yet to imagine who we are here. Or why. Ego is a gift to be enjoyed, and when the time comes to let it go, to let it go. OH lives in the tension among fear, hope, celebration and surrender, holding life lightly in his hands, as if it were a baby sparrow fallen from its nest, that soon will fly free. And shortly die.

BOREDOM, TERROR & CONVERSATION

Boredom is sham, a cover for fear and anger. And sadness. Given the kaleidoscope of reality that entertains our senses, above and beneath awareness, the idea that boredom results from tedium is ridiculous. Particle physics is only the latest to provide evidence that no micro-second can be retrieved, nor is it like any other. This reality provides more fascination than a single nervous system can engage in a single lifetime. The only way a sentient being could experience boredom would be to die. And honest brokers would have to admit to profound uncertainty about that. The closest any of us has ever come is what we call "near-death" experiences. And near-death experiences are as close to actual death as chocolate is to garlic.

[A possible exception is undergoing general anesthesia. I once asked an anesthetist if it was true that general anesthesia is as close as we come to dying until we actually die. "It sure is," he said, "We paralyze you, then put you on life support, hoping your body will take over again when we remove the life support." "No wonder," I responded, "we're all so scared of anesthesia." "Good instinct," he confirmed.]

Terror, on the other hand, is the very real, appropriate emotion in response to a full bodied, unfiltered encounter with reality. As in Zen meditation. Or war. Or sex. Or death.

You may know Noam Chomsky as a radical prophet, full of biting criticism of our nation's domestic and foreign policy. A tougher, meaner Ralph Nader. Our Hero first knew him as a linguist. And still does.

He's the champion of the idea that language is not something we learn from those around us, but is hot-wired into our DNA. Not so much the vocabulary, which we do learn, but the structure, what we once, if we are over 50 years old, called grammar. The structure of language. Though we may not talk in understandable language until several months to a year or more after we have been separated from our mother's womb, Chomsky says we're born, even conceived, knowing how to make sentences, hot wired for conversation.

And Chomsky is persuaded that the purpose of language, the reason it evolved in our kind, was not primarily so we could speak to each other. Chomsky on language triggers in Our Hero the idea that language is a tool primarily for sorting out what goes on inside us. The electrical morass, neurons firing in our heads, initiating action by our limbs and genitals. For the godlike task of trying to order our own chaos. We mainly use language to filter ideas, theories, feelings, emotions. What we know but perhaps didn't realize that we knew Not only physicists or writers, everyone. When we speak aloud we get a look at what has been cooking somewhere inside us. What percent of the electrical activity has ever been consciously perceived, in the most conscious being, a mystery no one has ever solved.

From earliest moments our efforts are focused on the dual task of knowing what is going on inside us, and trying to communicate it to others. You have spent a lifetime struggling, mostly in vain, to describe to someone, anyone, what you know. From your depths. Every now and again you seem to connect, surprisingly, intuitively, with another person, and you immediately want to penetrate, enter, merge with that person, to spend, extravagantly, your vital life force, empty yourself.

Intercourse. And it isn't a matter of whether it is sexual or social, verbal.

And why not? In the course of this story you will consider this mystery. And if OH manages to engage you, you will cease to chastise yourself for this impulse, this instinct to merge and devour the one who wakes your passion. Manage, maybe. Kill, never. The female praying (preying?) mantis dines on her mate after sex, surely for some survival purpose, perhaps to eliminate the possibility of genetic rivals. But the metaphor, for us, is about the desire to merge, to enclose within one's self, another being with whom one discovers empathic, sympathetic vibrations.

And maybe, when the encounter succeeds, we will feel the impulse to kill the other, destroy her because she has seen you. Known you.

No one has seen God and lived.

You will likely find it as frustrating as OH does, that even such a mighty merger, love-making, erasing for an ecstatic, consciousness-eclipsing moment the boundaries that mark your end and the other's beginning, that your beloved remains nonetheless separate, unattainable. Frustrating so long as we hold out hope, or expectation, that language, or for that matter fucking, can achieve the dream of merging with the One.

The mystics, of every age and religion, have sacrificed everything in pursuit of this merger. Our Hero has learned that to be alive, to swallow oxygen, is to be a mystic. Implicating us. Every one of us a mystic.

We brought nothing into this world and it is certain we can carry nothing out. And in that seeming despair in fact lies the hope. What we seem to acquire between being born and dying distracts us from the dream that haunts us. Ken Wilbur once wrote that whatever is not present in deep dreamless sleep is not real. We thirst for what spoken and written language cannot capture. What, despite the inadequacy of language to capture it, we know.

I would not wish you to think that Our Hero despairs of language, nor of finding pleasure, confidence, in the tightly packed atoms and molecules that lead us to call something "real". But he hopes you will hold the language of his story lightly, so that you may not confuse your projections onto him with some more objective sense of "reality".

Perhaps the chief illusion of the post-Enlightenment west is this notion of objective. For it would require that at least two of us have identical perceptions of something. And though we can't be sure, since so far no one has succeeded in entering into the body and mind of another, we can be reasonably certain that your electrons and mine are not traveling identical neuronal paths. Objective suggests exorcizing the subjective, and guess what—I, am the subject of my perception just as you are of yours. So kiss off objective. Whether or not you steer clear of the notion of post-modern, simple logic and basic knowledge of physics has eclipsed our confidence in the illusion we once called objectivity.

Feel free to dip in anywhere, at random. OH wanders through this odyssey and so may you. Because the words appear in linear sequence, it will seem as if you ought to start at the beginning and follow page by page until the end. My guess is that, if you do that, you will either quit somewhere along the way, or become angry at having to finish the book. Your choice. Mine? I'd meander. OH does.

ENTRY POINT

OUR HERO'S TECHNICOLOR

SELF-DISCOVERY

OH was persuaded by his friend and physician to celebrate his 60th birthday by scheduling himself for a colonoscopy. It was to be an intimate encounter with a part of himself he had lived within inches of all these years. Yet it remained to him a mystery as great as what lies beyond our cosmos. He had resisted, mainly because he felt taking such a look might be more penetrating and insightful than he was prepared for. Greater than his language and emotional maturity was sufficient to assimilate.

Not to mention a lifelong aversion dating from having his temperature taken as a child, to having anything put up his asshole.

He watched on the color monitor above his head. The startling pink peristalsis embracing the flexible probe as it made its way into his previously uncharted inner self, caused him to weep. The technician mistook his tears for complaint of discomfort. OH wanted to reassure him but what was he to say? That seeing these living fleshy cells, sheltered and so much fresher than the corrupted flesh he saw every day in the mirror, moved him to tears? So he shook his head when the doctor asked if he was in pain and the doctor presumed he was having a neurological reaction to the mild sedative they had given him. It was an experience of such intensity that OH momentarily forgot that for the technician and the doctor, this was routine. That they watch many such TV shows every day. He half expected them to express astonishment. Oh, the wages of the over-eager ego.

It's not only that outside language cannot fully express what we all hear inside ourselves, but that we become quickly and easily dissatisfied with our own words. When we release them from our thoughts into airborne audibles they are such a pale imitation of what we intend for them to carry. And to give vent to anger at our frustration seems as if we are reverting to infancy. The secret we hope to keep secret is that the frustration we felt before we learned how to speak, remains. Sometimes it is even greater than when we were infants because we sometimes think we will finally find words adequate to the task. Words are not up to it.

Infant, enfant, from the French, meaning not speaking, referring to the pre-verbal stage of a person's life. When a child cries we check it for hunger, pain and damp diapers. Failing to find any of these, we shrug our shoulders and guess; exercise for the lungs? Who knows. Perhaps it is this frustration, the motive behind every writer's writing. The drive to express what we know from our insides. John's Gospel in the Christian holy writings, calls Jesus, the Word of God, suggesting that even God is eager to say what remains sublime. So eager that God would challenge the Hebrew prohibition against limiting the divine being, taking on corruptible flesh. Perhaps, dear reader, you find this an arcane theological notion, but it makes the point. The wish to speak inner secrets knows no boundaries. And though the infant's frustration may be more obvious and less guarded than ours, ours is no less urgent. Imagine God's frustration, seeing how we respond to the divine attempt to speak to us. It unnerves us. We respond with murder.

If you wonder why we humans make war on each other while we all pray for peace, this is the reason. Boredom, the cover for our fear. If ever things seem likely to settle, we immediately begin to fear how they may, as they surely will, soon come apart. So perhaps Our Hero can precipitate the crisis before it precipitates him. If I cause, or at least precipitate the chaos, perhaps I can order it. Or bear it. The most eloquent expression of our deliberate creation of chaos, our drive to take charge of reality, is war. The moral equivalent of speaking.

So an encounter with his colon, more moving and demanding than a Dostoevsky novel, stirs OH to look into the world's womb, the salty sea, wondering whether it may yet yield the secrets for which he yearns and fears.

WHALES MAKING MORE WHALES

Before we tackle the ancient mystery of war, and the problem of evil, let's talk about the recovery of gray whales in the eastern Pacific. And what we humans might have learned from them had our curiosity been aroused a few centuries earlier. Before, say, the Iraq invasion. We advertise, not without cause, that it is due to the human protection of whales, banning the hunting of them, that they have gone from near extinct and human avoiding, to plentiful and human friendly. That grain of truth obscures an instance of our species myopia, regarding ourselves as the measure and determiner of all things. The whales were here long before us, and have a survival strategy more profound than ours. But, we say, our behavior toward them will decide their fate. A silly conceit. And OH has seen the even more certain reason there are so many of these beautiful beings. Gray whales, OH discovered, are sexy, like dolphins, arousing feelings in him not unlike the feelings he remembers when he first saw a photograph of Elizabeth Taylor in a red satin dress with the mounded tops of her lily white breasts exposed. She was then married to Michael Wilding.

You ever wonder why we do all this exploration, expend all this energy as if there was something missing, something we need to discover? Why wonder about the whales when we have scarcely scratched the surface of the mystery of our own brief tenure here?

Perfection, that awful longing, turns out not to be about something unattainable, but about our unconscious appreciation of things as they are. Of reality.

There is something grotesque, subversive, unpatriotic, un-American, about believing that life and experience as we taste it is sufficient. Perfect. Nothing needs be added or subtracted. If we all believed this the Dow Jones Industrial Average would have stalled at something under 1000.

OH has fallen asleep many a night wondering what sleep is. Is the reason we seem to need it, so we can surrender for a spell our drive to alter and improve the world? To surrender ourselves to the inevitable merge with the atoms and molecules in our orbit? As respite from the way he spent his day, struggling to rearrange them? He hasn't, thus far, formed a business plan for marketing this idea, for adopting a strategy based on things being perfect as they are. He has reserved a domain name on the internet for the day when he does. For reasons of national security, and in hopes of getting a shot at the next dot com spike, that name must not be revealed. Not yet.

Here's something that eluded Our Hero the 30 years he was a parish priest: Church Growth. Written in caps because it became an enterprise, an MO, one that was supposed to define at least one of the purposes of being a church. Get bigger. More people, money, programs. The American Way. It found itself a seemingly legitimate mandate in a passage known as The Great Commission in Matthew's Gospel, chapter 25; Go ye therefore into all the world and make disciples. That, in American terms, was the Mission Statement to which Church Growth was the Marketing Plan.

Had you known that OH was a priest? A parish pastor? Even after thirty years the matter of his ordination still came as a surprise to him, challenging his conviction that reality is trustworthy. This was it? The whole nine yards? What if he wanted more?

The whales. Ah yes, the whales. This warm up is suggested by the notion of big and bigger. Better and better.

Even though there may be some logic to the idea that getting bigger meant exposing more people to Right Thinking, it always seemed a contradiction to Our out-of-step Hero. If God is God (a hairy proposition, one admits), then the universe lacks nothing, right? Evolving, changing perhaps, but perfect. You mean nothing exists apart from God? (including evil . . . oh shit . . . see next book.) So what's our job? Job? To be. That's our appointed task. Being. And wondering. And sleeping at least a third of our tenure here. Sleeping in order to protect us from even more doing. The more we sleep the less damage we do.

Let's have another run at it. If God is God, there is no reality apart from God. And reality, whether or not we can track it, is utterly trustworthy, requires nothing additional. We are reality's servant, not its master.

OH has dedicated some portion of his curiosity to considering the notion that sleep is the activity that focuses our wondering. Asleep is when we do our most useful work. Our least destructive work.

Not that nothing is happening, but that we have nothing to add. Everything was packed into that sub-microscopic dot before the Big Bang (I know, where did the dot come from?). And has been expanding (unless it is contracting) ever since. What could be more fascinating, not to say satisfying to a true narcissist, than paying close attention to what happens to the bundle of matter that begins as a single cell made up of a microscopic egg and sperm, expands into a life, until it finally contracts back into a plethora of microscopic particles, and perhaps ???

So who's going to do the work, make the money and cook supper? Good question. It's One OH's wife has asked him, accusingly, at least twice a week for several decades. His sputtering attempts to describe a completed universe have cut little ice with her and driven him deep into his introverted chasm where he investigates the many incomplete explanations for what he knows and cannot communicate. Like, I hate to cook. I'll wash up. What if I burn the chicken? Reality is complete. Perfect.

Physicists tell us the universe is pretty much Nothing. What seems to be something is the nothing that looks to us as if it is frozen into a moment of stillness. It offers us the illusion of being something. Motion is what Everything is. So even the notion of a Perfect God, complete in God's Being, is a physical and philosophical contradiction. When we get to talking about the ocean (Our Hero uses place names even though they describe Nothing, illusions of Something), you will see what is meant by this odd fact. This something that turns out to be vibrating strings of no thing.

Oh yes, whales. Perfect beings, gray whales.

Our Hero has seen whales fuck. And didn't know for sure that's what he was seeing. And even today, a couple of years later, he wonders why it affected him as it did. It made him know he could die, feeling as if he had experienced everything his cells had organized themselves to experience. (The phenomenon we call dying will be addressed later.) For some period, whatever had been rearranged in him by the experience cut through his usual defensiveness and created in him a serenity so convincing, he nearly trusted it would last. In seminary he had learned the name for this tendency to attribute permanence to something one finds awesome: idolatry.

Even more than the birth of his own children—(he sired five)—watching whales fornicate persuaded him that regarding the world as in need of improvement was not merely mistaken, but stingy. Which turns out not to be as tragic as it first sounds, since, the universe lacks nothing—is in fact perfect. So redemption, the goal of western religion, turns out to be an unnecessary add-on. Like fins on a Cadillac. How would one redeem what is already perfect? And why try?

Another aside: the perfection ascribed to reality does not mean that reality is static, unmoved. Merely that reality, while in constant flux, is a process we neither can nor need rearrange. And we have nothing to add to it, except awe. And maybe gratitude.

Our hero's encounter with UR (ultimate reality) went like this: He was paddling out into the Pacific, due west from San Diego, in his sit-upon kayak, on a lovely January afternoon, hoping to see a great gray whale. They migrate by southern California for a couple of months each winter on their way from Alaska to the tip of Mexico, Baja California Sur.

OH became aware of another kayaker, in a sleek green sit-in boat, paddling 50 yards astern, off his starboard side. He waited for him to catch up and they talked as they paddled further from the shore. When he told OH he was from Brattleboro, the nearest proper town to the tiny village where OH lived in Vermont, he knew this was going to be an unusual day. The stars were lining up.

The green kayak guy spotted the pod first and they paddled hard to catch up to the whales before they sped off. It's a silly exercise because the whales know you're there long before you see them. They decide whether they're going to do commerce with you today or move on. But you can't help yourself. You paddle as if your life hung on whether you catch them. It feels like that. Like wanting to add value to reality's perfection.

When they were perhaps thirty yards from the whales, close enough to see the barnacles on their backs and catch a whiff of their strong rank odor, they stopped paddling. They felt a little nervous being this close, and a lot excited. They could see three whales lolling on the surface. One was smaller than the other two, but not a baby. Maybe a yearling.

The whales sounded and the two kayakers paddled closer to where they had been, figuring they would, as they generally do, sound and disappear. But as they came within 10 yards, the surface slick suddenly erupted in an explosion of water and whales, so violent they feared their boats might capsize and be sucked into the huge wet vortex. Like Captain Ahab. The three whales had their fins wrapped around each other. They came far enough out of the water so a third of their bodies were briefly visible. Then crashed down again into the ocean in a canon ball that drenched the kayakers and rocked their boats more violently than the biggest swell.

"Holy Jesus" the man from Brattleboro prayed aloud, as his green kayak rocked and rolled.

The two paddlers stayed there for close to an hour while the whales repeated this astonishing dance a half dozen times. Between leaps the smaller whale floated on the surface so close to them his eye seemed focused directly on the humans. The other two whales were on the far side of him, blowing and making that wonderful whale sound that one might think was groaning. But by now the kayakers suspected should be associated with ecstasy.

"What do you make of that eye staring at us?" Our Hero asked his companion. "Do you think he doesn't like our being here?"

"Have you ever heard of a whale turning over a kayak?"

Neither had, and they decided the whales could leave them any time they wished. Our Hero remembered thinking later that he would willingly have risked drowning to stay there. He took his uncharacteristic bravery as a sign that something in him understood this was about more than mere voyeurism.

(Some time after this conversation, OH came across a web site of a video in which a Japanese kayaker was hit and overturned by a killer whale leaping free of the water. Amazingly the kayaker, after a an anxious moment in which his fellow kayakers shouted to each other, surfaced, upside down and then righted himself. Soberly reconsidering his confidence that whales don't disturb nearby kayaks, OH came up with the rationalization that it was a killer whale, not a Gray, that did the dastardly deed.)

It wasn't until after they had returned and consulted with Scripps Institute of Oceanography that they confirmed they had visited the leviathans while they were indeed engaged in mating. But the two Vermont friends, by the time they had watched for a half hour, had little doubt what they were seeing.

Mating is fascinating, no matter which species. God's sense of humor is revealed in the logistics of mating, maybe especially mammal mating. We mammals seemed to have designed ourselves down the eons for many impressive feats, but mating still appears awkward. It's as if we had forgotten to streamline ourselves for this essential ecstasy. Even pigeons in the park, fluttering onto one another's backs, seem more at ease than we. And yet whales mating, the largest, most impressive species on earth, (or in the earth's amniotic fluid) as transporting a vision as any OH could recall, awake or asleep, was hardly streamlined.

The logistics are these: the mating pair wrap their fins around each other, maneuvering their lower parts in an effort to insert the male's legendary whale erection into the female's presumably equally impressive vagina. You've heard the expression, fucking in a hammock; well water is no easier a medium in which to achieve such precise positioning. So the younger male whale wraps his fins around the two of them and the three of them emerge from the depths in a prodigious ménage a trios. Their tail fins drive them upward out of the water, providing force sufficient for the coupling. They hurtle into the air and crash back into the sea.

Perhaps the physics of fucking make airborne ecstasy more intense than aquatic ecstasy?

Many mysteries remain. Each episode witnessed by OH and his companion lasted only a second or so. Is that how quickly they achieve ecstasy? Can ejaculation occur in such strenuous acrobatic circumstance? They saw six or eight of these leaps in the hour they watched. Does that constitute one session of love-making? Or do they climax with every leap? What about the younger helper whale? Is his role one of altruism or is there some reward for his efforts? Whales have been considered to be as intelligent as we, likely more, and they seem to lack the sense of shame or privacy about their mating that we think proper. What, if anything, might we make of that? Our Hero couldn't help but think that if his mating was half as heroic as theirs, he wouldn't be bashful, or maybe even private, about it either.

Perhaps this new genre of TV ads, for drugs to correct erectile dysfunction, were designed by people who had seen whales fuck. It is humbling for a human male.

And what, pray God, has caused our species to consider ourselves the crown of creation when we have been aware of our elegant oceanic companions for almost as long as we've been here? And might our arrogance not have been at least dented by the sheer size and beauty of whales? Apparently not, since we first greeted them with harpoons. Or perhaps that was, as Freud might have suggested, compensation, magna penis envy.

Or is that why we hunted them, to persuade ourselves, and maybe persuade them, that we could dominate them? Like attacking Iraq. It is a strategy long tried by our kind, this going on the offense when we feel defensive. A preemptory strike.

Since that day when the whales eyeballed Our Hero as they performed their mating with such extravagant energy, nothing, in the heavens or on the earth has impressed him more. The sublime beauty of the moment has, inevitably, lost some of its luster. After a period of unaccustomed confidence in his own perceptions, he finds himself again defending himself against his wife's accusations of laziness when he has failed to produce supper. And despite reassuring himself that he had seen what he had seen that afternoon, his verbal fumbling has left him wondering whether the mystic moment was of any practical use.

And the questions remain. Questions about our species and the way we seem to be ill-adapted to continuing indefinitely on the planet. And about our arrogance, again, at measuring everything in terms of how it includes us, as if we were not only the measurer, but the measure.

A cautionary note . . . Dissatisfaction has some purchase on reality. But since all is well, not **will be**, but **is well**, then dissatisfaction is serving some purpose. And even our species' unbreakable habit of searching for new ways to close out our tenure on the earth, species suicide, is surely, somehow, for God's perfect purpose.

Western appetite seems to have feasted on the idea of dissatisfaction. Surely, goes the thinking, it is our restlessness, our unwillingness to settle, that has driven us to accomplish all that we have. And, undeniably, something has caused us to do remarkable things. Though we may no longer have absolute confidence that Neil Armstrong's first cautious step onto the moon really was a giant step for mankind, it was pretty awesome. By our measure.

Or was it inevitable?

And then there is that leviathan, those whales. From what we can tell, they've been carrying on pretty much as they do now for millions of years. Haven't changed much, haven't accomplished much, at least that we can measure or appreciate. But they seem content. And what's that worth? What would you give for a moment's contentment?

Did you know this about ocean water—that it is close enough to blood plasma in its chemical makeup, that if someone has lost a large volume of blood and is in imminent danger of dying, you can transfuse them with sea water and keep them going for a while until you can get proper human blood into them?

Oh sweet Jesus, mighty Mohammed, beloved Buddha, what would it take for us to turn back to our mother, the sea? And let her embrace and nourish us, turn us from anxious weight bearing over-achievers to floating dervishes? Watching whales fuck came very close for Our Hero that afternoon. For a while.

Virginia Woolf, when she decided she'd had enough, filled her pockets with stones and walked into the water. Or perhaps it was when she decided she couldn't find enough here, hungered for a different sort of breath. OH had a recurring fantasy, driven sometimes by despair, sometimes by exhilaration, of swimming out from the shore, on the same trajectory as he had that day in his kayak, with the whales, and just keeping on swimming, until . . . Until what? He wasn't sure. Virginia Woolf. Suicide, yes, but not merely suicide. Also a serene return. Self-destruction or self-fulfillment?

Whales are more than merely a fellow species. And dolphin the same. Watching that television show about dolphins, meant to make us think they are cute and clever enough to do our bidding, put Our Hero off zoos and Sea World and animal shows altogether. Who gave us the right, he wondered (my God how OH wonders), to domesticate our fellows, like freaks in a side-show? That sea water is the earth's amniotic fluid, and the creatures that have chosen to remain immersed in it rather than emerge and battle gravity, seem not to have traveled as far from their origin and maybe from their roots. Or their souls.

Who will deliver Our Hero from this desire to demean his own kind?

Later we can wander through that minefield where matters having to do with the soul lie just beneath the surface, waiting to dismember our every conclusion. Our Hero is no Platonist. He doubts that souls exist. And yet he loves the conversation. But not here, not yet, not while we're still swimming with our close kin.

We know it is true that humans and animals have formed some sort of symbiotic bond over the centuries. Anyone who has ever lived with a dog knows that. (cats seem to beg the question somewhat) Swimming among dolphin and whales can wake up long dormant motions in us that feel so compelling we want to stay in the water forever. Small children, who complain bitterly when their bedroom is too cold, will stay in the ocean until their lips turn blue.

In San Diego you can swim with sharks. Leopard sharks feed on the plankton and crustaceans on the sea bottom rather than on flesh. On a warm summer day sometimes they are so plentiful just offshore that the curl of the waves is spotted rather than its usual blue/green. Some swimmers won't go in the water when they see them. OH feels as if he is being summoned into a sanctuary, a place of sacred serenity unequalled anywhere in the full gravity of dry land. The sharks are of course fantastic swimmers, so they usually get out of one's way easily. But occasionally they are so plentiful that one or more of them will brush against your leg or even bump into you, which, for OH, is like brushing by Julia Roberts in a crowded hallway. Their sandpaper epidermis as ecstasy-producing as Ms. Roberts' presumably silky skin.

La Jolla, California, like Italy's Amalfi Coast, is totally unsuitable for human habitation. Not only is there not a square yard of level ground, but the rocky cliffs overlooking the ocean, formed by seismic shifts still underway, are precarious and, at least to appearances, unstable. And those cliffs both in La Jolla and Amalfi are covered with houses. Big expensive houses. What in the nutty 90s came to be called McMansions.

In a rational world those cliffs would be bare. When Ellen Browning Scripps was trying to figure out where to build the first structure for what would turn out to be the world-renowned Scripps Institution of Oceanography, she chose a rocky site hovering high above the ocean. It provided a perfect vantage point for the work, but she also chose it because she was certain no earthquake-fearing person would ever want to build a house on so precarious and inhospitable a site.

Scripps must sometimes be tempted by the offers of billions of dollars developers would pay them for their land.

In fact there is an inverse ratio between the value of land and the precariousness of its location on one of those cliffs hanging over the ocean. The value of land in La Jolla is determined by its proximity to the ocean. Does it provide a peek-a-boo view, a stand up or a lie down view of the breaking surf? OH once took a job there, before he knew whether it provided work he wanted or was able to do, or paid a living wage. He accepted the job because along with it went a house with a lie-down, 180° view of the ocean. He liked the job well enough as it turned out, but that was secondary to being able to lie in his bed and see a whale spout.

It can get pretty primordial, this tight tie to the ocean and its seductions for us. Ask Monica Lewinsky what Presidential sperm tastes like. She's from southern California; she knows the thrilling, out-of-body, lusty taste of salty sea water.

An old joke goes: God caught Adam and Eve fucking in a pond in Eden. This must have been before the business about the apple because they were reveling in their naked coupling, not the least self-conscious. "Get out of there and stop doing that," God shouted, "You're going to make the fish smell."

We Americans spend billions in deodorants and perfumes to hide those salty smells. And we spend many more billions to be able to live where the tides and breezes carry those scents back to us. We are an ambivalent, afraid-of-ourselves species, as drawn as we are repelled by signals of the nearness of our origins. And where, do you suppose, is the most often chosen location for disposing of the ashes of our cremated bodies? Yes, the ocean.

Did you know that the weight of our ashes is roughly equal to our birth weight?

One more piece of evidence that you have been perfect from the start.

A person is what percent water? 60%? 70%? OH remembers vividly the first time he held a box of ashes from a cremated parishioner in his hands They were the ashes of a man he actually knew, had talked with, had cocktails with. Stood next to him at the urinal in the men's room at the club. And now he was preparing to toss his dusty remnant into the ocean. My God; this is what's left? Yes, of course. Fast oxidation. Cremation evaporates the water in us and the ashes are that part of us that isn't water. Not much. The weight of one's cremated ashes are equal to one's birth weight. "We brought nothing into this world and it is certain we can carry nothing out." When OH used to read that as he processed the coffin down the aisle, he wondered if anyone in the church besides him got goose bumps.

When the Episcopal Church revised its Prayer Book to make it more up-to-date, relevant to the contemporary world, that phrase was removed.

Perhaps it is no longer true that we brought nothing into this world and can carry nothing out? Or is that a subversive thought in a progressive free market economy? OH always slipped it in anyway. He loved the rush it gave him.

Drowning is reputed to be a sublime death, if you're willing to place those two words alongside each other. What you do when you drown (OH has come close at least once) is take a breath in which what you inhale is water rather than air. Your lungs fill with water, not oxygen, H_2O rather than O_2, and you begin a rapid return to your origin. Not so much ashes to ashes, dust to dust, but water to water. Odd, isn't it, that one missing hydrogen molecule could rearrange reality so radically? Or perhaps it is that the reality hardly needs rearranging for things to seem to us to have been radically changed. Perhaps it merely uncovers what has always been there?

We worry a lot, and wonder, whether we are managing our tenure on this planet well. And what the future will be. How long we'll be here.

OH heard a lecture at Scripps Oceanographic one year in which a climatologist revealed to rubes like him what apparently the scientists have known for some time. Drilling into the polar ice cap has shown that climate changes, when they come, come very rapidly. The earth's climate changes from relatively hospitable to our species, which requires relative warmth, to a climate that will support only whatever can hang out for 150,000 years in ice. And the change, dramatic as it is, can take place fast, in a matter of a few decades. What's more, over the past millions of years the earth has had ice ages of 125,000 years, followed by 10,000 years of mild melt. We are overdue for the 10,000 year period which has been so hospitable to us, to give way to the next ice age. No one seems to know why the change comes, but it does, always has, and, so most think, will again. Soon.

And we will become an archeological artifact of a brief moment in the geological history of the earth. Vaporized, one way or another.

Strikes OH as pretty good news. Because it suggests the earth, this profligate experiment out here in our corner of the universe, will likely outlast our hubris. And the stuff from which we are made, which came from cosmic materials, perhaps from comets hitting the earth, may take a run at initiating another such attempt somewhere. Fun to think about. It's not necessary for us to think in purely parochial terms, judging the entire history of creation by how hospitable it is to we humans.

Look around tonight, if it is a clear night, at the little slice of our solar system you can see. See any color out there? Remember the first photograph you saw of the earth taken from space? This tiny green and blue ball floating in the vast grayness of space. That one view was worth every penny we had spent on the space program. For the first time since we crawled out of the slime we could see with our own eyes what was at stake. At last we had the vision necessary for us to gain an accurate perspective of our place in all this. When the next ice age embraces the planet, it will look very eerie and white from out there. But some organisms will hunker down beneath the ice and miraculously emerge after the long freeze. And color up this planet one more time, probably many more times, before the sun implodes or explodes.

Dying, which you and I likely will do before our species goes totally extinct, is the measure of our hope. Think of it this way: in your mother's womb you were content to lie still, warm, well nourished, without ever drawing a breath. (This describes a healthy, happy pregnancy.) There are conflicting opinions about what being born is like and, while some mystics say they are able to recall their birth, most of us can't. Assume it's stressful—which seems likely—being squeezed, like a turd by muscular spasms of peristalsis, down the birth canal.

We often speculate that the biological purpose of birth being stressful and unpleasant is to provoke that explosive burst of protest that causes our lungs to inflate for the first time. Now we have become an air-breathing being, subject to the insult of gravity. Biologists are reductionists, calling all this the mechanism of survival. But who decided survival was to be preferred over quiescence? Seems a given, you say? Life over death? Stick around. If we are able, let's suspend our judgments about this matter.

"Always err on the side of life," President Bush said, explaining his motive for signing a bill to require another court to decide whether to remove Terry Schaivo's feeding tube. Sounds impossible to argue with. But is it? Or could it be an unexamined prejudice that stands between us and the full taste of being for which we hunger?

Jump to the close of a long eventful life. You are entertaining at least one terminal process. Organs have begun to falter, ceased to function as we count on them to function—the lungs, the heart, brain, liver, kidneys. The errand you went on 84 years before, with your birth complaint, has become nearly unsustainable. Your family is tortured by the sight of you struggling.

What they cannot conceive is that you are struggling, not to continue the task of exchanging gases, or to continue the effort to defy gravity, but to gain the courage to stop. The good news is that you will. It has been guaranteed.

Imagine each breath as a gift of oxygen, in return for which you offer a gift of exhaled carbon dioxide. One day, sooner than we imagine, there will come the most sublime moment in which you become willing to offer your gift, exhaling Co_2 without requiring another breath in return. You will have come to so fully trust the process of which you have been for a time a part, that you are willing to release your insistence on receiving anything. It is the moment for which you have been longing.

And you will experience ecstasy. Bliss. Find yourself in the same state as you did before you underwent birth—filled with fluid and freed from the effort of exchanging gases and carrying your weight under the burden of gravity.

Consciousness? Bet against it. Consciousness seems a condition of the struggle we call existence. And a condition the ego appears to insist upon to try to maintain its illusory centrality. But who knows? Let's just say it's hardly necessary and maybe even undesirable. But human beings have come to treasure it as the prize above all others, and seek reassurance that we can count on its continuing indefinitely. But once we are beyond the death grip of ego, for which dying prepares us, the issue of consciousness surely fades.

Our Hero has been present for several deaths, and not once, even of a young man who had been propelled from his motorcycle and rammed headfirst into a fire hydrant, was there a sign of struggle at the end. Every one of us can be certain we will relax into our dying; that is simply the mechanism, there is no other way to do it. If you watch it from some perspective other than ego, it looks rather like ecstasy. Surrender.

So why not suicide? Again, this is ego's insistence that it, I, am in charge. And whenever ego takes charge the outcome is not good. Because ego lacks adequate perspective, by definition, to choose well. Ego retains a parochial interest in what is a much narrower enterprise. Ego is a good observer, but less often a good actor.

Our Hero goes into a reverie, triggered by endorphins released in anticipation of his dying. In his reverie, dreamlike, his beneath consciousness is flooded . . .

But we're getting ahead of ourselves. Our Hero, while willing to complete his odyssey, has several adventures ahead, all preparing him for what he has been praying for. And the first, a long daydream about a matter that had presented itself to him long before his afternoon with the whales, becomes another reverie, fodder for the harvest for which he is being wonderfully prepared. He was taking a long walk through a Vermont wood, wondering if the neighborhood bear about whom he had heard but never seen, was, at that moment, observing him. Words, in an unusually orderly way, presented themselves to him like this:

Our Hero's Apparatus

Our Hero has long wanted to have this conversation with someone who would listen and respond without judgment. So today you're it. If you find this awkward or ridiculous, OH will never need to know. Just one of the myriad agenda he is eager to check off before he packs it in.

Stay tuned for OH's somatic reverie . . .

Now about my penis . . . I've never been really comfortable with it. It seems odd to me, almost unnatural, an awkward appendage flopping around, getting jammed against one leg of my pants so I have to root around, trying not to draw attention as I rearrange its position. Every now and then it escapes through the fly of my underpants and rubs against the pants fabric, or worse the zipper, and I have to turn aside and push it back so it doesn't get rubbed raw, a most unpleasant sensation that can last for days.

Not that I haven't learned how to cope; I have, but not without wondering if every guy spends energy like this.

And I've never been really comfortable in men's locker rooms either, not only because I worried that my penis is unimpressive. I try not to look at others, not wanting to compare, but most men, most of the time, seem to me to have larger penises than mine. Not all the time. That's one of the weird things about a penis; it changes size and shape. Not only when it fills with blood during sexual arousal. Some days I can hardly find it, as I stand in front of the urinal, groping through my fly opening. Others it is fully 30% larger. Just one of the mysteries about a portion of my body, this one always seeming too embarrassing to discuss. Until now.

I once visited a nude beach which turned out to be a gay nude beach, a mostly black men's gay beach. It soon became clear that the reason these men visited the beach was to display their penises. I had no idea the male organ existed in such dimension. Those men must have to have their clothes specially tailored. And while I have been told that women find large penises a turn-on, surely there must be a limit. These were limp, not erect and they hung to their knees. I mean it was awesome. But where would all that go in intercourse? I have never felt my equipment inadequate for the sport of making love. It has, except when it betrayed me, and went limp, always expanded to a size more than adequate to reach the cervix. What could be the use of more? Sort of like those multi-million dollar salaries for CEOs one reads about; what would you do with all that?

Do you suppose whales concern themselves about this? Perhaps if it was customary for us to accept the assistance of a smaller, younger person to achieve the awkward acrobatics of fucking, we would be less self-conscious about our penises.

Self-consciousness, self-awareness, our post-Freudian prize, is sometimes the booby prize.

It's a long hike, through these Vermont woods, strenuous and hilly, and the reverie gathers steam . . . from penis size to money . . . OH has an active, fertile, self-accusing mind. And an ego that sometimes lets down its guard.

I wonder if I would think about this if Freud had never lived. I wonder if Freud worried about the size of his penis. I suspect the issue is more than one dimensional. I always feel lonely in locker room conversation. And wonder how many others may. I never remember the names of the San Diego Chargers players. I sometimes take part in conversations about the economy and the stock market; I know the language of that world pretty well even if I have no confidence in my opinions. But I live in fear that someone will ask which stocks I like or even which I own. Since I sold all the IBM stock I inherited, I never have any idea, what's in my portfolio. I take the monthly statement from its envelope and look at it (sometimes only checking the bottom line), and I drop in at my broker's office an average of once a week. Nonetheless, I don't feel I know any more about what makes a sound investment than I did 40 years ago.

The best and worst moment since the dot com collapse and the undermining of our national hubris since 9/11/2001, was when my beloved financial counselor was, in a fit of post terrorist traumatic stress, moved to acknowledge that he has no idea what makes a sound investment anymore either. It's sort of like my telling an anxious parishioner that I really have no idea if there is a God. Or what happens to us when we die. Sublime moment of human intercourse. Discomforting intimacy. A moment of honesty perhaps best reserved for a drunken or death-bed conversation.

(Narrator's Note: No, we're not off track. OH is confident you will see how the locker room conversation about stock portfolios, and the preoccupation with penis size, are about the same matter.)

It may be that every guy in the locker room worries about the size of his penis, and his portfolio. It's a pretty sure bet that even the world's savviest investor can't predict the future. But in the moment I always fall for their seeming confidence in their predictions. Do you suppose they detect how intimidated I feel?

I don't know. Maybe if I had an impressive chest and a buff body (I have been told I have good legs), I'd still care about my penis. I suppose when you think about it, it makes good sense that it would stand in for your sense of yourself as much as anything. I mean, we're still animals, still have the drive to replicate our DNA, so why not focus on one's penis? Where the DNA is housed, or at least makes its exit. Women's breasts, though their utility in child rearing is obvious, don't seem the exact equivalent. Maybe that's why women seem to feel safer exposing glimpses of their breasts than men do showing a little of their penis. Aside from porn, I've never heard of a line of clothes that exposes even a tiny part of the penis. A shadow of the shape perhaps, beneath a fold in the trousers, but never the actual flesh. No equivalent to a mound of breast bursting from a halter top.

Listening in on OH's subliminal conversation can often take you places you might consciously by-pass. OH not only seldom by-passes even his most eccentric inner musing, he never passes on an opportunity to listen in on those of others. He takes it as a side-mission to restore eavesdropping to a place of dignity.

Our Hero once overheard a conversation at a sidewalk café in Hollywood that caused him to consider the matter in a new way. A young man described to his attractive lunch partner, a slightly overweight but beguiling young woman, his having gone to a neighboring bar on the prior Thursday. It was the night of their Big Dick Contest. The winner (the overheard conversation didn't provide enough information for OH to know precisely how this was determined) drank free for the night.

"A really cute guy came on to me," the man explained to his friend, causing OH to realize that she was not his sexual partner (although these matters of sexual identity and choosing had become much more slippery in his lifetime). "He kept feeling me up and everything. But he was just too weird for me."

Our Hero came to full alert as he considered what might have made someone at a Big Dick Contest too weird for the tastes of a fellow contestant.

"I could just hear my therapist," the fellow continued, "chastising me; 'Why do you draw such tight little boundaries around yourself?' But I didn't care; weird is weird."

Some will say, OH knows, this is another sign that we have lost our way, detoured around the basics of survival and flourishing, and are soon to be extinct, if not as a species, at least as a productive nation. But he wasn't sure. He wished to wonder more, whether there might be something subtle at work here, something that might either show our unconscious awareness of the nearness of the next ice age, or of the futility of trying to manage our own future.

Sexual exploration, while fraught with danger in this time of AIDS and STDs, still somehow struck OH as a sign of growing courage in exploring our origins and our destiny.

And he reminded himself that he was in California, predicted by nearly everyone to become an uninhabited island if the magnitude 9.3 liquidizes the earth before it refreezes.

Hear then a parable: "The juvenile sea squirt wanders through the sea searching for a suitable rock or hunk of coral to cling to and make its home for life. For this task it has a rudimentary nervous system. When it finds its spot and takes root, it doesn't need its brain anymore so it eats it. (It's rather like getting tenure.)" From *Consciousness Explained* by Daniel Dennett, p.177.

Perhaps the only thing scarier and more threatening than ignorance, facing the unknown, is knowing. Every discovery, down the road, when the thrill of the lusty first moments has receded, becomes part of the warp and woof of daily existence. This is true not only of biblical knowing, of sexual intimacy with another person, but of knowledge of the universe around us. Moving from the thrill of lust to the wonder and comfort of true intimacy requires a trip through boredom. And boredom, as we have already seen, is a cover for terror. The terror of knowing, and of being known.

An article in **Harper's**, February of 2003 as I recall, described the author's visit to a NASA facility in New Mexico that tracked not only satellites we humans have hurled into orbit, but the countless other objects flying through our air space. It seems they began quietly looking for these things, meteors, comets, in the 1960s. They have been amazed at the numbers of them and at the number that have and will eventually collide with earth. We humans, like the juvenile sea squirt, have, believing that we have found a permanent and imperishable home, been munching away on our brains hoping we have no more need for them. (As evidence, I cite the level of political discourse in the nation.) Some in NASA (do you suppose they wake the President to tell him there is a comet that looks to be on a collision course with earth?) have the bad luck, and bad jobs, to know this rock on which we have taken up residence, is not so safe. So, seeing that things may not be as secure as they seem, it has been incumbent on them to cease from devouring their brains. Unlike the rest of us, they must continue to live under the discipline of active thought.

The surest way to devour your own brain, says OH, is to station yourself in front of the TV. Some believe watching high caliber programming will postpone the brain ingestion, but OH has concluded that Marshall Mcluhan was right when he focused on the medium rather than the message. Long before cable, satellite TV or the internet, the Canadian seer said the medium itself would be of greater consequence than the content it carried. And OH, himself a recovering TV addict, knew Mcluhan was right. Every time he reached for the On button on the remote, he called his friend Zach, his sponsor in their personal 12 step TV recovery program.

His sponsor would tell him to get up and leave the room, walk outside, even in the cold of winter, inhale deeply, exhale twice as long through the nose, walk back into the room where the TV was, unplug it from the wall and go into the kitchen and make himself a cup of tea. It often worked. And equally often didn't.

Those geologic ages you learned about, that they track by digging though layers of earth, finding the different sediments of rock and fossil at different depths . . . you must have wondered what caused one age to end and another to begin. Well, the people at NASA have now concluded that many of the changes, particularly the sudden, catastrophic ones, were the result of big space rocks running into the earth. Though they don't talk a lot about it, there is consensus now that the mysterious and rather sudden extinction of the dinosaur was a result of something big hitting the earth. What was not wiped out in the initial explosion perished over the next short period, from starvation, as the layer of debris from the collision obscured the sun and made all the vegetation die. All but a few species disappeared.

And we're on course now, whether from a new ice age, a collision with a meteor, or perhaps a nuclear exchange of our own making, for species change, for the slate to be wiped clean for a new beginning.

And what has this to do with my self-consciousness about my penis? It has everything to do with what self-consciousness is. And does. Since we worship our consciousness, regard it as the wondrous thing evolution has been working toward the past many millions of years, when we talk about life after death, it is the possibility of the post-corpus survival of consciousness we mean. Though I hate to rain on our parade, it falls to me to alert you to even our beloved consciousness as a sometime-event, soon to be terminated. It was not an inevitable outcome of evolution and we must so far admit to being agnostic about consciousness having some permanent place in some realm or dimension beyond ours.

When OH described this to a friend and said he found it good news, his friend agreed.

"It would be a shame," he said, "a huge letdown, to discover it had all been about us after all."

Somewhere in the ether my self-consciousness about my penis is preserved. Like the information on the hard drives of those computers that had been trashed and then picked up by a charity that would recondition them and give them to people who had no computers. MIT sent some young geniuses to examine them, wanting to find out whether the information seemingly discarded really was irretrievable. The computers were castoffs from companies and individuals and had been carefully cleansed of all data before being thrown out. When the hard drives were explored by those MIT whiz kids, a huge sum of data was found intact and easily accessible.

Though we don't yet understand the mechanism, it seems likely that every thought, conscious and unconscious, being a form of electrical energy, having utilized and altered matter, continues to exist somewhere in some form,. And if so, will, eventually be able to be retrieved. Good and bad news. All the concern about privacy of communication on cell phones and email will seem insignificant when the ability exists to pull stale and ill-considered thoughts from the air.

[As I was editing this, a piece came over the internet about a petulant remark Prince Charles made about the press, being picked up by a microphone. He was sitting between his two sons, at a ski resort, smiling for the cameras, unaware that one of the cameramen had a mike that could detect a whisper at a hundred yards. We can all expect to be tracked as closely as poor Prince Charles, our every thought as well as spoken words, once we gain the ability to pluck electrical activity from space even more easily and routinely than the CIA today listens to Osama bi Laden's conversations.]

OH is considering starting a lottery on the internet for people to bet on how far this effort will go before the inevitable extinction event. He has yet to work out how the winner will claim the Grand Prize, an extra nano-second of conscious existence.

In every exchange no matter is either created or destroyed. We learned that in fourth grade. Do you believe it? That there is a constant amount of material and energy in the universe; it gets altered but never added to nor subtracted from? Pretty conservative place, the universe. But remember, it doesn't all stay static, retain the same form.

Big Bang. So how did all that stuff get stuffed into that infinitesimal dot, so kinetic that it finally couldn't contain itself and burst its bounds? What made it explode? What a mess it must have made in the previously unblemished universe. And has been making ever since.

One day OH overheard his middle daughter say to his youngest daughter, "Everything was pretty good around here until you came along."

That God damn explosion keeps causing trouble, just when we think things are about right as is. Seeming, even if it is working with a constant amount of stuff, to innovate. Maybe the universe isn't so conservative after all.

The western United States are finally breaking into open warfare over the rights to water. Southern California, where millions have chosen to move because it's sunny and warm, and doesn't rain. That little pineal gland in the pre-frontal lobe, loves all that light. Despite the semi-desert climate, Los Angeles and San Diego have enjoyed plenty of water thanks to the Colorado River and the snow melt from the high Sierras.

Things got dicey in the 1940s and 1950s when the Imperial Valley became the center of vegetable growing for the entire country and much of the world. The Imperial Valley is a natural desert. So, tough lawyers did combat over water rights and worked out a deal that would let the farmers have the water they needed to irrigate and the cities plenty for their needs. But then chilly people from Chicago and Peoria, living long enough to retire for a long period, moved to warm places. Phoenix and Scottsdale, and Las Vegas and Reno became the fastest growing cities in the nation, and Colorado became not only a great ski resort, but a desirable place to live. And the Colorado River ran through those places. And all those new people needed water to live.

So now there's a new war on, and it promises to be not unlike the Arab/Israeli conflict that periodically threatens to engage the whole world. The only way there will ever be enough water to sustain the number of people the Big Bang keeps spilling onto the planet, is for the ice caps to melt and raise the sea so high that the seaside places that bring the highest rents now will be once again canyons for the dolphin to play in. Even though that water will be salty, unfit for drinking or irrigation, it will have taken some significant number of us to a watery grave. Or aroused our warring energies when there was insufficient land or potable water, so we will have practiced our ancient favorite, war, the incidental triage our kind favors.

There's no cause for cynicism about all this. We have been doing the best we can with what we have. But it turns out to be inadequate to save us because we have never been in charge and never can be. We may inadvertently extinct ourselves as we work to solve the dilemma of too many people for the water or the fossil fuel needed to sustain us. Every species makes self-defeating moves when desperate. It's not a moral failing, just an inadequate survival mechanism. Or, if one likes to think in terms of purpose, perhaps this impulse is built in to protect the earth herself from any species that seeks to dominate her?

Perhaps, as some are suggesting, what we mean by this ineffable name, God, is the universe, this marvelous, miraculous burst on which we have feasted for this season of humanness.

Ah yes, the gender issue. And fecundity. OH always had female dogs. They seemed easier, less aggressive and territorial, didn't lift their legs on the curtains. But he lost his heart to a black and tan male terrier, and discovered another dimension or so to the gender mystery.

Having the females neutered is strenuous surgery. Having the male neutered was barely noticeable, at least to OH. The terrier seemed OK with it also.

OH was fascinated to learn that when we are first conceived, a zygote in the womb, our gender is indistinguishable. We are androgynous for at least the first seven weeks, before male or female chromosomes begin their work. Then changes set in. Surely we retain some memory of this, however deeply buried. This always made OH feel better about discovering that he has what we now refer to as a strong feminine side.

And it caused him to wonder about his choice of vocation. He remembered hearing the dean of his seminary laugh at a student who complained that people don't treat clergy like normal people.

"We go to an archaic school called a seminary where we study documents the rest of the world has ignored for centuries, in languages no longer spoken anywhere in the world. Then we kneel before an authority figure the world no longer understands, nor, by and large, even recognizes, in a position which, under any other circumstance would be considered a sexual posture of submission. He lays hands on our head and confers on us the invisible power of what we call God's Holy Spirit. We dress in ancient dress, that today is worn only by women, stand a full head above the people to whom we are speaking, telling them what to think and how to live, pretending, hoping to know the mind God about all this. And we complain that we aren't treated like normal people.

After a decade in this vocation OH delivered a paper to a group of his colleagues, all male (it would be several years before women could be ordained), and suggested that, in our gender-confused culture, we clergy could, if we were willing, offer ourselves as role models.

We carry a male authority and a female affect. Since the clergy in those days were terrified of the gender confusion they carried, no one wanted to discuss it with OH. But every time he robed or disrobed in the locker room, or robed in the church vesting room, he wondered. Like his colleagues, he seldom passed up a chance to tell risqué jokes or use scatological language, demonstrating his solidarity with other males in clearer male roles. But he always wondered.

In the meantime, though we may have wrung out the penis issue until it can offer no more, we never stray far from its implications. And in the meantime there is more than enough to keep us entertained, and that is what OH hopes to do with you. To engage and amuse you with what you already have. Because, if you want more, you better die. You see, so far as OH can see, this is all there is, here.

And that, OH now understands, also applies to his concern about his penis.

BUILDING BIGGER BARNS

"What would you say," OH asked his spiritual advisor, "to a week in which a man's dog was castrated and he sold off his entire portfolio, worth well over a million dollars?"

"I would say," she responded with no hesitation, "the man was well on his way to Nirvana. Bliss. And his dog as well. Sometimes a dog can be released from the burdens of squandering energy in search of a mate, spared the demands of extending his genetic line."

And can a man, seeking the illusion of dominance, or hoping to stretch his claim on existence beyond his years on earth, be set free of his illusion by dumping his portfolio?

Depends. What's he to do with the proceeds? There once was a man who had a prosperous farm. [This teaching is borrowed wholesale from Jesus. Jesus didn't work it as hard as OH will.] Problem was his harvest was too big for his barns, even after he had sold all he could. So, smart man that he was, he built bigger storage barns where he could keep grain that would last through another season, insuring a surplus even if the next season's rains didn't come. He was very pleased with himself, even though it took him most of the summer to build the new barns.

The night he finished his final building he fell into a deep sleep. An hour into the sleep, so wonderful that he felt himself letting go of himself, he began to dream. You may remember falling into a sleep that deep when you were a child, almost like floating on a rolling sea. The man was well into his dream, a dream that was formless, without content but nonetheless filled him with emotion. Not exactly an emotion he could describe, like happiness or sadness, anger or ecstasy, but even more evocative. In his dream he looked down and saw himself lying on the bed. He felt a deep and unfamiliar sense of compassion for the person he was looking down at. His compassion combined with sadness that was as wonderful as it was unnerving. It was then that he understood that he had died. Perhaps we could keep the question of his ongoing consciousness at arm's length, just for the moment.

"Why, I'm dead," he intoned.

"Uh huh," he heard an affirmation that he couldn't identify.

He saw his bulging barns and began to laugh. He loved it that he could laugh like this. He felt himself losing himself, maybe the way the shuttle astronauts who blew up felt themselves flying apart. No pain, physical or mental. No regret or urgency. A weightless floating. Ecstasy.

"This is like falling asleep. Only better, easier." He felt a stirring in what he would have once called his loins, as if he was sexually aroused. Only now there was no ambiguity, no performance issues, only a sublime sense of merging. He understood he was about to merge, blend into everything, so his ego, his selfness would fade. And it felt fine. No, more than fine—he experienced ecstasy.

Watch from his perspective. (Well, not exactly his perspective because it was no longer his nor was there a him to have perspective, but we're going to continue to track what he "knows" as best we can. That tracking requires us to use language that involves making marks on the page even though the marks are inadequate to represent what it's like for him now.) Maybe you'd be willing to float along here, let your insides be informed by what your outside finds preposterous. If not, well, don't fret; we'll get back to you.

So, he sees the wonderful, brief appearance of our kind on the earth, the way we might see a Miramax Film about Lewis and Clark's trek across the part of our continent no European had ever made. He sees the whole thing. The weird little lizard-like creature that emerged from the stormy ocean and tested its lungs in air. The tentative foray of our near ancestor who was on earth with the dinosaur and who perished when the comet collided with the planet. He doesn't see it exactly in sequence; he sees it all at once, including the way it ends. Though he can't say exactly whether that huge cloud that shuts down history, as we have named our odyssey, was caused by a nuclear exchange or another collision with space debris. It no longer seems important. It's beautiful. Perfect.

Best of all, it really doesn't matter to him. His ego having been appropriately tamed, watches, spellbound. But not bound up in the outcome. The earth remains, even surrounded by that cloud obscuring the sun's light, even with a fraction of the species that occupied it when he was alive, even with the polar ice caps seeming to claim more and more of the earth as they meander toward the equator, still the most fascinating and beautiful thing in this part of the solar system.

What a trip! And how did this begin? Oh yes, it was when he'd brought in his bumper harvest and filled his barns to overflowing, and exhausted, lay down to get some postponed sleep. What a sleep! No one would want to wake from such a sleep. God knows he didn't. And his prayer was answered. He never woke.

Here's what he sees when he looks at the coasts of the various continents. The edges of the American continent, what had been known as the United States, goes under first, because, curiously, the most people had clustered there. And, like his bulging barns, the fabulous success of those who were able to live on the continent's edge, had become a liability in the sense that they were the first to go under when the seas rose. If that was a liability.

From his perspective he can see that those people have a funny sort of advantage in their disadvantage, one they likely would have given up if they had the choice. That was, they went first. And they tasted ecstasy early while their fellows in the middle of the continent continue their struggle to escape its embrace. Ecstasy has a strong, irreversible embrace.

He laughs; this laughing is new for him. Not that he never laughed before, but it was always careful, measured, conscious, chosen laughter. This was of a whole different order. This laughter is triggered by seeing himself, throughout his life, subtly backing away from the embrace of his mother, his first love, his wife, his children. Hanging onto himself. Now that he is experiencing the embrace of ecstasy it makes him laugh, spontaneously, to think that he once worried and struggled to avoid being swallowed by the embrace of all those he met so cautiously in life.

This was like being a sperm—swimming, darting, chasing, racing other sperm. But instead of its feeling like a contest to see which will reach and merge first, it feels like one of those bouncing air games he'd seen at school fairs, that you went into and when they turned on the column of air, you floated, lost control of where you were going, bumping into each other, laughing. That's what this watching is like.

Along with the sadness. The sadness, too, is of a different quality.

"See that guy over there in the corner, the one who looks lost, wandering aimlessly in a tight little circle? Uh huh; that's me. I thought

I was supposed to do something, be someone different, something more. And I never knew what it was. Watching now I see that's what I was there to do; wander. Wonder. And I did. But I never gave myself to it, never let it fully embrace me. Doesn't much matter now,; it has somehow come out as it needed to. And the sadness is like a necessary trace element in the reaction. The reaction can perhaps happen without it. But the outcome will be slightly different. This is perfect. So I'll give it the sadness."

Once he was walking along the spectacular vista by the Cove in La Jolla, California—birds roosting on the cliffs, body surfers boldly catching waves that dwarfed them so they seemed to be pieces of flotsam. There were always lots of people milling around on the shore, basking in a vintage Southern California scene. As he passed the west steps going down to the Cove, he overheard one sentence of a conversation between a young swarthy man, perhaps Latin background, and a fair-skinned Anglo. The swarthy one said, "You understand that God put me there because of the fucking shit I did." And the Anglo nodded; he understood.

Karma.

OH Revisits His First Kiss Revealing The Origin Of His Fear Of God

There once was a girl—beautiful, golden-haired 14 years old. The high pink color in her cheeks could be understood as blushing if you saw her once for only a moment. But if you spent time with her you would see that is her natural coloring. So beautiful. Her eyes, clear, blue, set in her head like diamonds. Her body the perfectly proportioned body of an athletic 14 year old. If only I could make you see her. But if I did you would have to be where I am, and I know you're not quite ready yet. So the best I can do is invite you to revisit someone in your own life at about that same time. You will understand.

"Her name was Jo Anne and her older sister, Lily, was my big sister's friend. Lily and my sister thought it would be cute if they brought us together. Their family lived on the Navy base at Sangley Point, across Manila Bay from Pasay City where we lived. I had seen Lily from a distance at school but had never spoken with her. My sister said she was going to have Lily over for the day on Saturday and thought she might invite Jo Anne if I was going to be around and would enjoy that. I remember trying not to seem too enthusiastic. And in fact I wasn't. Only because I thought I might not be up to whatever my part in such a day might be. We all went to the International School, and saw each other every day, but I had only longed for a conversation with Jo Anne, never actually dared initiate one.

"Sure, why not?" was as enthusiastic as I dared sound at the suggestion. So my sister set it up.

Our driver took us to the Army-Navy Club where the launch dropped people from Sangley coming to Manila for the day. As the sailor helped Lily and Jo Anne from the launch up onto the dock, Jo Anne leaned forward to take the big step up. Her scoop neck blouse fell away slightly from her chest and I caught sight of her budding breasts. Have I mentioned that we were in eighth grade? I guess you could have calculated that from our being 14. Just the very tops of her breasts, you understand, the place where her tan line from her bathing suit ended.

And my only recently testosteroned penis sprang into readiness. I had to turn aside to keep from being suspected of the sex-crazed boy that I now was. All three of the girls appeared not to notice. Fifty years later I still wonder how aware girls were in those days of the physical dislocations experienced by boys in heat. The jokes—are you carrying a knife or are you happy to see me?—wouldn't become common currency for several decades.

As we made our way to the car I became aware that my sister and Lily had talked about this and made plans. My sister got into the front seat of our Buick Road Master, black top, white below, four holer. Lily, Jo Anne and I got in the back, Lily on the passenger side, Jo Anne in the middle, me behind the driver. Jo Anne's thighs and mine brushed lightly so long as I was able to hold my right thigh up straight. When it tired, it leaned against hers. And I felt her left thigh push against my right one. At least that may have been what happened. It was the closest I had come, closer than I dared imagine, to sexual intercourse, and my body was way more ready than the rest of me, the rest being my psyche. There I was, sandwiched between my desire and my faltering courage.

When we finally reached our house, Lily and my sister disappeared, announcing that they would be gone for at least an hour and then we could have some lunch.

"Maybe you could show Jo Anne the cave beneath the house," my sister suggested.

I didn't dare look at Jo Anne, whose party dress had become in my mind a replica of the red taffeta dress Elizabeth Taylor wore in a picture of her I kept in my bedside drawer.

"OK."

Underneath our house was a 10 meter cave in which, so we were told, the Japanese made one of their last stands when the Americans liberated Manila at the end of WWII. It was a dirt cave with some primitive wiring and a couple of bare light bulbs at the entrance. As you walked toward the back, it became dark.

I rose from the couch where Jo Anne and I were sitting and started down the steps to the lower level where the cave was. Jo Anne followed. Neither of us spoke.

When we reached the bottom step, I turned to her and said, "It's a little dark when you get inside, so you better take my hand." I held out my hand. She grasped it. Had I not expected her to have a warm, flesh palm? My knees trembled. We walked inside. "The Japs held out here," I said. She said nothing. I turned to say it again, thinking she might not have heard me. Her full body was suddenly pressed against mine. Fifty years later I can almost pull back her scent, feel the brush of her cotton dress against me. I leaned my head forward and our lips brushed, then pressed hard against each other. Our hips surged, bringing our pelvises together and there we were, just like the movies. I felt her tongue lick against my tightly pursed lips and tentatively parted my lips. Her tongue found mine. For a moment I thought I might pass out. She cupped her hand against the back of my head pulling me harder into her. Feeling my erect, dancing member pressing into her, I pulled my hips back. She pressed hers forward. Our tongues wriggled inside each others' mouths like newly unearthed worms.

As with every species, we need not be taught some things. Unlike other species, our bodies are ready before it is convenient.

Who knows how long we were like that? Seconds to a minute or so, I'd guess. I had no idea where it might go from there. I remember thinking, since I was the male, it was surely up to me. So, thinking I was being polite, thoughtful, I stepped back. She smiled and held my hand tightly, seeming not to mind that mine was dripping sweat. We walked back to the cave's entrance. I wondered what I was supposed to do when we emerged from the cave. As I have done ever since, when in over my head, I demurred.

"Oh God, Jo Anne," I said as the harsh tropical daylight blinded us both, "I'm sorry. I didn't mean to do that."

I suppose she might have looked confused; I have no memory of what she looked like.

"It's OK," she reassured.

And now I know that it was. And much more than OK. It was great, momentous, natural, important. Forty years later I had an email conversation with my friends about our earliest sexual experiences. Great thing about email, these conversations we'd never have had face to face. And to my chagrin, they were experimenting, without qualms, from younger than Jo Anne and I were that day.

Do I regret this? No, not really. It was the fullness of what I was ready for at the time. The reasons that body and mind took so long to get in synch remain mysterious. And I am so happy that in these post-pill days our children seem never to have considered that allowing themselves to experiment with what their bodies are urging them on to do is anything except the best course.

A sublime moment in which even OH can now see the fullness of life completed, wanting for nothing. He can still replay the scene as if he had a Tivo in his brain, which leads him to understand that the producer and director of the scene have signed off on it. Given it their blessing, and it is ready for prime time.

OH finds it fascinating that these seemingly obscure moments somehow take on powerful symbolism, meaning beyond their significance at the time they took place. Imagine, dear reader, that there are perhaps a dozen such moments filed in your memory's hard drive. They reveal volumes about how you see yourself in the world. One great gift about being old is to replay those moments, now rich with meaning, no longer embarrassing. And OH wonders where Jo Anne is now. What might she look like as a 65 year old woman? Does she remember that day? That cave?

One day while walking his terrier along the shore (we're stepping aside a little here), OH saw a school of bottle-nosed dolphins racing through the sea, just beyond the breakers, leaping into the air, flipping, splashing. The terrier was intent on finding a place to do his business, pulling on the leash, but his handler was mesmerized by the incredible sight of a fellow mammal reaching speeds up to 30MPH out there 50 yards offshore.

So what? Well this: if you want more, then you better die. This is all there is, here. It doesn't get any richer than this, here. Our cousins, bottle-nosed dolphins, acting out our most exotic fantasies, the water a more-welcoming medium than land, swimming as fast as a cigarette-boat, maneuvering so perfectly they never run into anything—not even a swimmer in their path. OH is frozen in fascination. As mesmerized as he was that day with Jo Anne.

Dolphins and adolescents, showing themselves to be fully evolved Buddhas, an insight that convicts OH of the insight that each moment, each breath, is complete, lacking nothing. Perfect.

OH marks these moments as unscheduled encounters with his shadow. Wherever you go, the Master has said, there you are. Shema Yisrael. Hear O' Israel, the Lord our God, the Lord is One. Jo Anne and the dolphins—inseparable.

This is it.

All's Fair in Love & War . . .
And In A Herd

He wished to go to the movies. She had worked a long hard day and, though she would welcome the distraction, wasn't sure she had the energy to go out. He had lectured himself the hour before she came home, not to push her. He was, after all, retired. Sure, he had vacuumed the living room, fed and walked the dog, cleaned out the cat's litter box, done the laundry, folded and returned it to the drawers. You see, he was piling up points; he wanted to go to the movies. He'd even gone online and picked one out. She was tired. She still had a job. Still earned money.

"OK," she relented, "let's go to the movies."

"No, it's OK to stay home."

A lying stalemate. Name-callers title this "passive-aggressive." Both knew it. They'd been here before. Often. Both were reluctant to fight for their desire. They had another run at coercing the other into making the decision. Finally she took the bolder course.

"I really want to go to the movies," she said with some conviction; "let's go."

So they did. But now he was angry. Not that he was ever cleansed totally of anger, but now he had something to pin it on. He liked having a reason. Free-floating anger, with no specific trigger, felt somehow illegitimate. She had prolonged the indecision, so he thought, until it was almost, not quite but almost, too late. Now she needed to find her glasses and her Senior Citizens Pass. He stood silently, sullenly by the door, poised. Pissed.

They went through the door at 6:50 for a 7:05 movie. Just enough time, driving recklessly, to reach the theater and get into the 20-people-deep line at exactly 7:05.

"We're late, as usual," he muttered.

"Sorry," she said, graciously, sincerely.

He muttered something more, something, luckily, neither of them could make out. There was only a single ticket window open at the Cinema 12. The ticket seller an Afghani with marginal English skills was slowly deciphering customers' requests.

"They always have a lot of previews," she consoled.

"Fuck," he muttered, embarrassed to admit that he liked the Previews, that he loved the colors and noise blurring across the big screen. Trailers for movies he'd never go to, but he got to see some of the violence and sex at numbing speed. She pretended not to have heard his favorite swear, the one with the double stop.

A second window opened, this one with an American-looking woman adjusting her headset so she could speak with movie goers who might be potential terrorists and couldn't get to her through the bullet-proof glass. He rushed to be the first at the new buying opportunity. He arrived at the window simultaneously with the man in the leather jacket who had been at the front of the line they had both just left.

"You have to get in line," the man said to him, testily.

"I was in line," he protested truthfully.

"No, in the place in line where you were," the leather jacket man persisted. Neither the leather-jacket-man nor OH himself perceived that OH, although he had been lining up since nursery school, had, in his building agitation, quite lost his grip on the basic working principle of a que.

Now, OH is a peace-loving man. In fact he had a minor role in the peace movement that was presently experiencing a futile rebirth, stillbirth really, in a pyrrhic effort to head off the President's determination to unleash the full arsenal of the greatest power ever assembled on earth to punish the weird Arab who had tried to kill the President's daddy a decade earlier. OH had written several eloquent pieces exposing the idiocy and hypocrisy of the President's war intentions. He thought he might even evolve from a minor to a major peacenik. Especially if, as he anticipated, the war would soon get underway and lots of innocent civilians would be killed and featured on CNN. He had, decades earlier, been a minor peace celebrity in the small Midwestern city where he lived during Vietnam days.

So he was quite unprepared for his warlike response to the man who pointed out to him the error of his line-jumping ways at the Multiplex Cinema 12. Just as he pulled back both hands with the unexamined intention of driving them forward into the other man's leather-clad chest, OH's wife put her body in harm's way between the two of them and shouted:

"You're wrong! You jumped the line!"

Luckily, in the habit of obeying her, especially when she raised her voice, he took the fateful step back. And the conflict was avoided. Not the Cuban missile crisis perhaps, but nearly as unnerving to OH. It was an assault on his picture of himself.

"What is up with me?" was the thought that ran through his mind like a mantra while he tried and failed to be distracted by the movie.

And the answer was that he had been above ground for six and a half decades. He possessed a nervous system that had served him admirably for perhaps five of those decades. And now the insulation that was designed to enclose the cables through which electrical signals passed, determining when he would walk, breathe, swear, fight, flee and sweat, were beginning to fray. Like pieces of old hemp. And the signals that once passed smoothly and efficiently through those cables were sometimes short-circuiting on their route from brain to body.

It was his good luck to have married a wife who was several years younger who had a kinder, gentler work career that had not stressed her cables so severely. And their years together had conditioned him to listen to her. Which spared him potentially worse consequence than the damage the encounter did to his sense of himself.

He was, he recognized with a mixture of sadness and relief, no longer a suitable leader of any peace movement.

Seahorses

I wonder how much you know about seahorses. Though it is a stretch, there may be something here that could redeem a man's ability to retake his place in a peace movement.

Some time ago OH's beloved wife suggested that they break their normal Saturday morning routine of vigorous exercise (truth was they both suffered from repetitive motion injuries, not from work but from having been alive so long that everything they did, walking, eating, lying down, they'd done so often it had worn deep furrows in their muscular and nervous systems, fraying their wiring) and go visit the aquarium to see the seahorse exhibit. Though there was a time, not so long ago, when they both would have considered such a passive Saturday morning activity the first step onto the slippery slope of extinction, both now entertained sufficient aches to yield.

And they had it on good authority that the seahorses were awesome.

How awesome can a creature be that is no bigger than your great toe? A rhetorical question to anyone who has suffered from the gout. The answer, however, is anything but rhetorical.

Seahorses, as it turns out, occur in all the oceans, but not plentifully. They are not flourishing because of their popularity, especially in Asian cultures where they are regarded as having varied magical healing powers. In the middle of the exhibit at the aquarium a video was running, over and over, of a woman marine researcher looking at a pile of dried out seahorses.

"I can't believe I'm seeing this many seahorses all piled up in one place like this," she emoted, every 30 seconds. "This is more seahorses all in one place than I've seen in my research all over the world." The exhibit was arranged with the video of the woman being interviewed in the middle of the room, surrounded by small tanks with live seahorses. So OH and his wife heard the interview repeated over and over as they circled the room.

They believed her the first and third times they heard her say it. The eight and twelfth time their sympathies went to the pirates who had dried out the seahorses to grind into powder as an aphrodisiac. Their growing petulance with the whining researcher, alas, provided them great insight into the environmental sensibilities of the Bush administration. And with a less than compelling sense of the urgency of setting aside Asian sexual satisfaction for the sake of the tiny beguiling creatures.

But the reproduction part of the exhibit changed everything about their attitude. By now they had seen seahorses of various size and appearance, including two species that looked for all the world like seaweed. Until they took a closer look and saw, tangled in the spinach, more creatures like the others they had been watching. Baby seahorses. Now they were hooked.

Another video—this one of seahorses fucking; at least that's what they supposed they were watching. The lovely miniatures met at mid-abdomen and seemed to move in a fashion reminiscent of an Asian porn film, with erotic dignity. OH and his wife watched this video even more times than they had the one with the hysterical biologist. This was not one of their own kind, no feelings they ought to avert eyes. It was in fact mesmerizing. Tiny orange smelt-like eggs being transferred from one seahorse to the other. On the fourth viewing they realized the transfer was from the female to the male, exceeding the most radical vision of Gloria Steinem. That alone would have caused them to stand transfixed, watching again and again. And these creatures were so, well, stately.

Once again, living proof of God's sense of humor in the drama of reproduction. Only, in the case of seahorses, the humor was really fun, thrilling, not slapstick or self-conscious as it is with our species. They looked better designed for it.

These seahorses provided no opportunity for salacious observation. And for OH and his beloved this was a life-altering experience. Why that should have been so is a matter about which they were curious, but not openly so. Their insight into their own sexuality, likely as developed as most late adult humans, nevertheless lacked keen self-understanding. And had for nearly seven decades. They had adjusted to the likelihood that it was not likely to yield now. But that in no way lessened their fascination nor respect for the subject. They remained open to new ideas about the matter.

The video must have time lapsed ahead at this point. The documentation on the wall said nothing about the gestation period. The next scene, in living color, was of the male going into what appeared to be painful, acrobatic labor. OH and his beloved, with many of the specifics of birth familiar, after five live births between them, wondered, aloud now to each other, whether the male seahorse produced the hormone Pertussin to initiate labor, as the human female does. OH put his arm around his wife's shoulder and drew her into him. She didn't resist but neither did she reciprocate in any way.

"I love you," he whispered.

"Of course you do," she responded. "Anything less would be monstrous."

The video proceeded until, with one huge seemingly agonizing contraction, the seahorse, the male daddy seahorse, spewed a dozen micro-seahorses into the surrounding water.

Now you understand why the seahorse will be here when our human descendants have surrendered their grip on existence. We used to call it swinging from both sides of the plate, a derogatory remark, not a statement of awe, certainly not admiring of a species interested in perpetuating itself. We say the seahorse is endangered and it may be. But think about it; the seahorse has devised a way to bypass what we consider biological necessity. We, on the other hand, cannot even figure out what to do with the things of which we are inordinately proud. Plastic, computer terminals, shopping bags, developments that lent to the United States winning two World Wars, are now choking us as they are our former enemies. And the American President, eager to make sacrifices to the plastic gods (to whom all of us pay homage), has outlawed genetic counseling by his minions, severing yet another chance for us to become as creative as the seahorse. And, believing he is bowing to biblical mandate, he has declared his determination to return all matters of reproduction to the management of male hierarchy.

Word has reached us that the fifth cloned human baby, whose origins are in cells scraped from its father's inner cheek, has been born in Australia.

Consider the seahorse.

Because we are unaccustomed to considering the planet's future without our kind, imagining that would be a tragedy, may we pause to sit quietly, marvel at the seahorse and reconsider?

You'll recall the scene from the movie, "The Graduate" in which the older man, offering his most valuable advice to the recently graduated Dustin Hoffman character, says the one word, "Plastics." And the audience laughed, not because it was so ludicrous but because, though perhaps banal, it was good advice. Yet even as we understood that a young person seeking his fortune would do well to focus on the future of matters plastic, some unconscious, infant gene in us also knew that we were designing our own demise.

Freud and Darwin combined to persuade us that the strongest drive in any organism is the drive to reproduce itself, to give its DNA the best chance to survive and flourish. But consider the possibility that, as some biologists have suggested, a form of altruism may exist that actually motivates one to put the good of a greater number ahead of its own future. Yes, we are a part of a particular species and surely we do have a strong interest in the good of that species. But suppose our species has taken a turn, or several turns, which can lead only to results that diminish the prospects for, say, the future of the planet—and the extinction of many species, in addition to ours.

Is it possible that we, unconsciously perhaps, might put the survival of the planet ahead of our own survival, if the two interests look to have became mutually exclusive? No, this is hardly a logical matter, but looked at logically, what would it benefit a species to insure its own survival only to lose the very platform on which the species stands? Or sits? or lies?

An upgrade of the archaic question—what does it benefit a man to gain the whole world and to forfeit his own soul?

One evening OH had dinner with friends who were now five years out from one of life's most wrenching crises. That night five years earlier, while they were dining on pheasant and champagne, they discussed the possibility of the NASDAQ going to 10,000 in the next couple of years. If you were not there you may find such speculation ridiculous, but those of you who remember an allegedly astute analyst predicting the Dow touching 20,000 before the new millennium will hardly find the conversation anything out of the ordinary.

All four people remember it now, vividly, five years later. The host had suddenly gained a death grip on the edge of the dining room table.

His body went rigid and his previously sophisticated, multi-layered conversation dwindled down to only two words, "yes" and "no," spoken over and over, in a monotonous inflection that would have annoyed his vivacious wife had she not looked into his eyes and realized that some significant part of him had gapped it, escaped, left.

"Are you all right?" she queried, stalling, already knowing the terrible answer to her own question.

"Yes . . . no," he explained definitively.

"What's happened?"

"No . . . no . . . yes . . . no."

And so it continued until she called their friend and neighbor, and sometime physician (though they had discreetly gone to another physician two years ago after a New Year's neighborhood party at which heroin and some group sex had eroded their confidence in their neighbor/doctor's judgment, and they found the prospect of stripping naked in his office had taken on a new dimension they couldn't cope with).

He came right over, was sober and professional, took one look at the husband sitting like a department store clothes mannequin, and diagnosed, "He's had a stroke." And called 911.

For the following three weeks the husband said only no and yes, reminding his biblically literate wife of St. Paul's admonition, "Let your yes be yes and your no, no." But try as she did, she was unable to discern, despite his perfect enunciation of each of the two words, whether their usual meaning applied. And just as she was about to sign the papers to have him declared incompetent and make arrangements to place him in a facility that smelled like urine and cost more per month than their mortgage payment, as she explained to him what she was doing, the way she explained to the dog that she would take him out as soon as she finished the paper, he spoke a third word.

"Maybe."

"God damn it," she said, not because she wasn't excited to think that his speech ability had just increased by a significant percentage, but because she was caught off balance. She always hated it when he surprised her. "Did you just say 'maybe'?"

"No . . . yes . . . I mean maybe."

And from that moment his recovery became what everyone agreed was miraculous. He regained virtually all of his physical movement, though those who knew him well could detect a stiffness that wasn't there before.

And he shifted to eating and writing with his left hand (in fact he took to wiping himself with his left hand following a bowel movement, something his wife nor anyone else ever knew and which, if he had been asked, he would have described as the most difficult transition he had to make). But he regained his command of business, took back the helm of the venture capital firm he had started a decade earlier, learned to drive again, and even went back to playing golf, though his handicap shot up 10 points.

"So that's your handicap now," his business partner laughed one day as they were playing golf with a client, "29?" I'd kill for that handicap." (He was seeking to impress their client, their biggest investors, that not only was the head man whole, but they could even laugh off his brush with vegetabledom.)

We meet these people five years after the stroke, at dinner with OH and his wife.

Stroke man: "Have you got an evacuation plan for you and your family in the event of a terrorist attack?"

OH: "No." To himself: "Are you shitting me? You could only say two words five years ago, were suitable for adorning a chair into which you needed to be strapped. And you're spending your precious conscious energy planning how to skip town after a dirty bomb?"

That thought gave way a few weeks later to a serious consideration. Though not of a suitable egress from the city, even though it provided sanctuary for the biggest naval shipyard on earth. And its sumptuous suburbs the highest tech firms that housed experiments in science-fiction-scary germ warfare like those the President accused his hated Iraqi opponent of harboring. He proposed to remedy this threat to human future by launching cruise missiles and other even more exotic new tricks for teaching lessons to the newly annihilated.

For OH it was reminiscent of sophomore year in college when he and his friends had spent an odd Wednesday afternoon drinking coffee in the student union and listening to radio reports of Soviet ships with missiles on their decks sailing closer and closer to American warships with orders from the charismatic young American president to intercept them. Years later, when trying to pull back his emotions of that moment, OH was unable to say whether the jokes and bravado, the black-humor banter, was bull shit or resignation.

Now he watched the president's remarkably clear image from the Azores. The president was younger than OH and unconvincing in his attempts at projecting gravitas. (Though OH understood he in fact had the power to end the Big Ballgame right here and now . . . which perhaps constitutes the mother of all gravitas?) OH found that his being in his mid-60s caused him to feel less anxious than he had in his mid-20s when he had last waited while a president played chicken with our continued existence.

Two days later, home from the Azores and his lonely conversation with the British and the Spaniards, his two remaining allies, the president, this man who so recently was telling raunchy jokes in the locker room of his Midland country club, is going to talk to us again. And OH has given up trying to play tennis in a southern California gale and gone into the exercise room where he discovers that President Bush's image is about to appear on the TV bolted to the ceiling above the machine that builds your abs. So, for the first time in months, after conscientiously avoiding doing so, OH watched as his president worked to persuade the nation he was worth his big salary.

He found himself fascinated by the staging of the president's talk. Having closeted his television when the networks began Counting-Down-To-War-With-Iraq several months earlier, he hadn't seen the President's image in a long time. Remember when President Clinton (remember him?) used to speak to the nation? To explain why he'd received a blow job at work or lobbed a few cruise missiles at the tent someone had told him was the meeting place of Osama bin laden (remember him?)? Clinton was always seated at his desk in the Oval Office. In fact that had become the signature of a president coming before his subjects in an historic moment. JFK and the Cuban missiles, Ike and Little Rock High School, Bush and Gulf War I. OH knew Ronald Reagan appeared from there but he's damned if he can remember for what crisis. Always the Oval Office with the windows behind showing the Washington Monument, the flags standing on either side of the desk. One always strained to see what he had on his desk, and in the book cases behind and to the sides. Clinton's photos of his wife and daughter were, OH assumed, meant to reassure us that Monica's blow jobs, while unseemly perhaps, were not going to split up the First Family.

So here comes George W. Bush, walking, hands by his side, down a long corridor toward the camera and a podium. He walks dead center down a red runner that stretches from the far top of the TV screen to the foreground. He is wearing a blue suit, jacket buttoned, flag pin in his lapel. His hair has been recently styled into the attractive wavy pattern of a serious yet charismatic leader.

Why have we abandoned the oval office and the desk, the Washington Monument? What can this mean?

This president is a vigorous, activist man, not a sedentary passive man who sits to deliver hard news. He is young and athletic, in charge. And so he projects. Except for his slightly quivering lower lip. Am I, OH wonders, the only American who sees it? The president's voice echoes oddly, metallically, like the halting voice of someone who has learned to speak through a tracheotomy.

"Is it because I am old," OH wonders, "and have seen inside my decaying self, that I actually feel compassion for this man as he promises me that he is fulfilling his oath to protect me? Not safe. I know he has no more ability to protect me than I do to protect him. And I understand that he really would like to. And if he can persuade me that he can, maybe he'll even begin to believe it himself."

On September 11 two years before, OH initially thought the news people were nasty to report his wild cross-country meanderings, raising the unspoken possibility that he was afraid and running away. ("Why didn't the President return to Washington immediately?" Ari Fleisher was asked. "Because there were credible threats to Air Force One and the White House.") I mean the man is President and we have just absorbed the worst attack on this continent in our history. Of course he's afraid. Weren't you?

OH was in the barber's chair in a storefront in Jacksonville, Vermont, population 467. The barber had a 12" black and white TV on which she and OH watched the second tower swallow the airliner, like a fire-eater. He thinks he remembers that she never stopped clipping his hair.

"There aren't enough of us up here for them to bother with," was the summary of what he remembers her saying. The only other thing he remembers either of them saying was when she told him the price of the haircut, $9. It seemed like a lot at that moment.

So when President George W. Bush flew his zig-zag course cross country that night, touching down at various Air Force bases, OH felt for him. Now, watching him stride purposefully to the microphone in what he assumes is an often rehearsed approach. He will announce to us that he is going to make war on the evil dictator, OH has to discipline himself. He reaches deep into his most Buddhist bag to practice the compassion that will override his anger and cynicism. This man, OH reminds himself, The President of the United States, (POTUS to the Secret Service) is feeling the moment in his lower colon.

What then shall we say of God? If the President, a more conscious stand-in for God than the Queen or even the Dalai Lama, has to run to the toilet after standing steadfastly before us at the end of a long red carpet, what is left?

Nothing.

That which is not present in deep dreamless sleep is not real. (Usually attributed to Ken Wilbur.)

You may remember the story of the woman who answered a knock on her door and discovered God standing on her front stoop.

"May I use your bathroom?" God asked.

"But aren't you God?" the woman asked. Who wouldn't ask?

"Yes," God answered, "I am who I am. And that's the problem. Your door is the tenth one I have knocked on looking for a bathroom I can use. Everyone assumes God doesn't have to go to the bathroom, so no one would let me in."

Maybe that's why President Bush stands instead of sits when he's got something scary to tell us. Maybe he can keep his sphincter shut better. I've had that experience. No doubt you have, too.

On his 60th birthday OH received a card from a friend, The card offered three pieces of advice to those over 60.

1. Never pass a bathroom.

2. Never trust a fart.

3. Never waste an erection, even if you're alone.

The president is not yet 60. But we all know how that office ages a person.

The president calls himself a person of faith. Newsweek magazine ran a photo of him on its cover in which he had his eyelids pressed tightly closed, presumably praying. Though one could mistakenly believe he was straining to produce a great thought. Or perhaps a BM.

Aside from renouncing his family origins—patrician Connecticut, Phillips Andover Academy, Yale—one wonders just what our President means when he calls himself a person of faith. He told a gathering of evangelical church leaders that he really should be sitting at a bar in Midland Texas rather than in the East Room of the White House. "Had I not found God," he told them (I quote from memory), I would be a drunk, not here, as President." (The equivalent, he may have thought, of John F, Kennedy's meeting with the Houston Ministerial Association in 1960 to reassure them that his decisions as President would not be bound by the Holy Father in Rome),

And though he probably did not mean that every person who "finds God," would gain such high station, his statement holds a clue to what he thinks faith means; the avenue to a "good life." Perhaps he even thinks the decision for faith—for it is clear that in his view the direction of the initiative comes from the human, not the deity—causes one to fall into divine favor. If you want to know who has faith and who does not, you look at how the person's life is going. Happy, successful, responsible? Must be a person of faith. Failure, problems, unhappy? A person lacking faith.

It doesn't wash. No one has a faith more fierce than Osama bin laden.

If and when the history of this period is written, the question of whose faith prevailed will depend on so many things we cannot know right now. What I suspect is that the two principals in the battle they both believed to be Armageddon, George W. Bush and Osama bin laden, had like personalities. Each believed he was appointed by God for this moment. Each pronounced, as if God's prophet, the other as "the evil infidel." Each announced that the forces of history, guided by God's hand, would carry his side to inevitable victory.

In their pronouncements and their attacks on each other, the two warrior/leaders were acting out roles appointed centuries before. Though those opposed to this war used rhetoric that made it seem the United States was, as Osama bin laden pronounced, the great Satan, carrying out the malicious intentions of the commercial predators of western capitalism, when viewed from the perspective of history, it will surely look more as if the United States, with her sidekick England, was simply living out her karma.

Having become, by weird accidents of geography and history, more powerful than any nation since perhaps Rome at the opening of our era (CE for Common Era), we could not have escaped the hubris, the temptation to overreach. As President Bush made nearly explicit, to see ourselves as doing God's bidding.

And then there is the matter of our unconscious wishes. Why, a reasonable member of another species looking on might ask, would a President or a Prime Minister want to commit his young people, his nation's future in the flesh, to the slaughter of war?

A woman I know—smart, sophisticated, self-aware and thoughtfully opposed to the Iraq war from a more principled position than most—told me she happened to have the television tuned to CNN when the shooting began. She said she sat in front of the set for an hour and a half watching the extraordinary pictures of a war in its beginning stages. She described becoming gradually aware that she was feeling excited, had an adrenaline rush. Horrified at her own emotions, she turned off the television and went to bed.

But she couldn't sleep, because she now understood why we humans do war. She understood with her own nervous system, could feel the excitement in her body. And she knew all the reasons it was a bad idea and could lead only to grief.

Until and unless we become willing to own those impulses and wishes in us that we know are unacceptable, self-destructive, we can have no hope of their loosing their control over us.

Since OH tested out that idea on some email co-conspirators, he has received hate mail. Deservedly. "I hate violence," one offended correspondent protested, "I certainly have no fucking interest in offing anyone."

So there.

Which brings us to the issue of inside information. Information that is inside one rather than outside. The question about such information is not whether it exists, though that remains a legitimate wonder, but whether anyone can discern and describe it accurately. Can there be an objective focus to such a subjective dimension? Can I describe to you my inner life—thoughts, fantasies—with confidence that you can conceive of what I am speaking? As opposed to reflection, which you will recognize as auto-intercourse which, though scorned by many, may be a way to meet a more agreeable companion, and an entirely defendable venue for seeking reality.

OH, who has been ordained longer than he hasn't been, believed, like his mentor Alan Watts, that ordination, like confirmation, or even initiation into a fraternity or Boy Scouts, must certainly be accompanied by an epiphany of some stripe. Watts describes his confirmation in the

Anglican Church during his schoolboy days in England. The endless tedious lectures about the history of the Church and the silly stories about Christians being eaten by lions, he and his classmates assumed, must be a cover for whatever the real secret was that would be revealed at the critical moment.

They learned that each boy was to have a private meeting with the school chaplain prior to the visit of the Bishop who would lay hands on them for confirmation. They suspected the secret would be revealed in that meeting. So they all waited in the room of the first boy to meet with the chaplain, and when he returned, they pounced on him, all asking at once what the secret was.

"Well," the boy said, "Father Bliphin talked mostly about masturbation." (It took a couple of the boys a moment to realize that "masturbation" was "beating off.")

"Father Bliphin actually talked with you about whacking off?"

"Yep, even more than about Jesus."

So, they decided, that was it. Something about being Christian was enclosed in the practice that consumed more time and energy among those boys, who had all recently reached puberty, than any other. And for those whose testosterone rush had just begun, it either spurred them on or gave them something to look forward to.

But we have strayed from the matter of inside information. Well, not really strayed, because the question remains, or rather two questions remain: is there such a thing? And is it possible to use language to describe to someone else what has gone on inside one's self?

PAIN AND INNER KNOWLEDGE

When OH was engaged in hospice work he became close friends with a doctor, a Roman Catholic Nun, who was fascinated by the matter of pain. Here we are speaking of undeniably inside information. Who hasn't had pain? Surely among the most subtle and elusive matters modern medicine has tried to address.

When we encounter a person lying on the ground screaming, crying, veins visibly pulsating, holding tightly to his bleeding leg or his head, we would all agree he was in pain. And most of us, perhaps not all, would have some idea of what that might be like. But what makes us think we know? Is the pain I have experienced identical to what this person is experiencing?

"Describe the pain to me," most of us have heard a doctor say, if not to us, to someone nearby. And some, few, can be quite articulate. "It is very sharp, located just above the ankle, a burning sensation, throbbing with each beat of my heart."

Helpful words; at least a transaction is taking place. And, so we would love to think, the doctor may have heard enough other people use the same words so as to recognize something familiar. And be able to make a good guess as to the pain's cause. And intensity.

But more likely the doctor is stalling for time, hoping the pain will subside. If it does not, the doctor may give the person some deadening agent, though that often is considered a bad idea until the cause of the pain is known. But the issue remains—has the person described something one can recognize, with confidence,?

Can you measure your pain? Against what standard? Have you ever doubted another person's complaint about their pain? As if it were a play for sympathy? Is that because you have done that yourself? And when you did, was there at least some pain to start, even if less than you made it out to be?

OH is attracted to the idea recently introduced to him by a friend who has been treated by Dr. John Sarno. Dr. Sarno believes that the vast majority of pain has its origin in a mechanism once recognized and acknowledged, now mostly discredited along with so many of the ideas of Sigmund Freud.

Dr. Sarno believes we all have issues lurking in our unconscious. He likes rage; OH is drawn to shame. These are matters that our conscious mind would find deeply disturbing. So, when they begin to seep (or do they jump?) from the unconscious to our conscious, our brain executes a maneuver, a kind of feint. It fakes one way, to throw off our conscious, and then it goes another way. The brain chooses a place in our body that is vulnerable (it seems, classically, to be the lower back for Americans) and starves it slightly of the oxygenated blood it normally supplies that spot. We experience pain, which distracts us from the rage or shame that threatened to become conscious.

At first OH found the idea whacky. Who would choose being in pain over facing some emotion like rage or shame? But the more he considered it, the sounder it seemed. Dr. Sarno, unlike Dr. Freud, does not believe one must undergo talking therapy in order to "deal with" the unconscious threat. All that is needed is to acknowledge that this is in fact what is going on. Having failed in its subterfuge, the brain will begin to restore normal oxygen flow and the pain will recede.

OH has, quite literally, an Achilles heel. His plantar fascia tightens up and causes him exquisite pain. OH has, under the Sarno canon, faced down his plantar pain a number of times, discovering the underlying demon from which his brain wished to distract him. He hit the wall on the matter when a nine-year-old daughter of his next door neighbor was killed in an accident. OH and his terrier were big buddies of the little girl, and when his plantar fascia began to throb, OH welcomed the pain rather than wrestle with it. He acknowledged that, at least in that situation, his grief was in fact greater than he was willing to bear. He would embrace the pain instead.

Though this is a work of fiction, not a diagnostic manual, OH invites you to give it a try. Or to check out Dr. Sarno on the web. If it doesn't work for you, sue Dr. Sarno, or Dr. Freud. Or your meddling brain. Before we're through, the man is going to reappear and rearrange more than just OH's head.

Pipeline to God and Prayer
A Religious Experience

Here's an experience common to ordained clergy. A person says, "Would you pray for my sister who has cancer?" What black-heart would say no? "You have a more direct pipeline to God," they will say.

Now in the sacramental communions, ordination has to do with function. The priest is ordained to preside at the Eucharist, or, in the case of a Bishop, lay hands on for confirmation and ordination. What about in the confessing communions, where the sacraments are not the focus? Well, perhaps they are set aside for preaching and for healing. Preaching because they perhaps are articulate, carry authority well. And healing because they understand the nature of ease and disease better than most.

What about that pipeline?

OH would never have dared to present himself for three years of seminary, let alone ordination, unless he had persuaded himself that he had a direct encounter with God. In a moment I will describe that encounter, but first, understand that this tradition, of a direct and verifiable calling from God, has deep historical roots in American religion. In the Massachusetts Bay Colony one could not own land until one had a conversion experience which was told to and approved by the elders of the Colony. It is the origin of what we still know as a land covenant.

OH, once he had decided ordination was for him, worked as hard on behalf of confirming his divine calling, and with as much fear and trembling as any doctor ever did in learning human anatomy.

Freshman year in an Ivy League university, he lived on the third floor of a large, walk-up dorm, with an under-aged roommate who would, 25

79

years later, expose OH as a religious fraud. It would prove a more than adequate payback for the many nights OH returned to their room knee-walking drunk and threw up.

On the night in question, a Sunday, they were both sober and doing work in preparation for Monday's 8am Spanish class. His roommate heard the voice calling first.

"I think someone's calling you."

He listened and it was true. He looked out the window into the soggy quadrangle where a few geeky freshmen were ignoring the rain to practice the new sport of Frisbee. He saw a friend, not his closest friend, wandering, drunkenly in an erratic pattern and calling out his name. He wondered what the significance of this could be when his roommate, not yet his enemy, suggested that he ought to go down and check it out.

He did. And set in motion, on that rainy fall Sunday evening, a chain of events that may have been preordained or could be seen as a set-up for a lost young man who was feeling the pressure to figure out what he might do to earn a living.

The actual events unfolded in this way.

"What's the matter, Jeff?"

"I don't know." Jeff wiped his eyes and his nose, both running freely. He was wearing a sweat shirt and khakis, no raincoat, and even though it was only drizzling lightly, his clothes were already soaked and dripping. He appeared to neither notice nor care. "I was talking with Suzy and she said something to piss me off and before I even knew what I was doing I ripped the phone out of the wall (remember when phones were firmly fixed to the wall?) and threw it through my window."

OH remembered his mother saying, "In a crisis, staying calm is the most help. If you can go for a walk, all the better."

"Let's walk for a while," OH suggested. Jeff didn't respond but when OH began walking toward the arch leading out of the quadrangle and onto the city streets, Jeff followed. They walked the streets of the city for an hour or more, talking very little. Jeff began to sober up; periodically he whimpered like a puppy that wants to be let out. OH touched Jeff's shoulder lightly to reassure him and Jeff would seem calmed.

OH looked up and saw a red door; many of the churches in that part of the city had red doors and he supposed that's what this was. He climbed the steps and tried the door. It was unlocked. Jeff followed wordlessly. The two of them walked into the church which was dimly lighted, had collegiate seating, bench pews facing each other across a long aisle extending the length of the nave down to the altar that was draped with a colorful brocade cloth. Above the altar hung a lighted lantern with red glass. OH remembers the dank church feeling medieval and mysterious. And just the right place for the two of them to be for that moment.

The two boys/men slowly walked half way down the aisle and up a step and sat on one of the hard wooden benches. Later OH would say he had no idea how long they sat in silence, but he was certain he experienced an eerie, unmistakable calm in himself. And Jeff seemed to sense it too. OH who, though he had been brought up in the Episcopal Church and spent five years in Church boarding schools, had never made heads nor tails of what religion was about. He knew nothing of how it worked. But some impulse, hard-wired from his boyhood, directed him to reach into the rack in front of him for a Prayer Book. He discovered the same book he remembered from all those early years. (It was a book that was to survive only a few more years before revision.) The book fell open to a page on which, even in the dim light, his young eyes could make out the words of the Lord's prayer.

"Our Father who art in heaven . . ." he began. And the two of them said the Lord's Prayer from memory. OH flipped the pages and came upon a Psalm; "I will lift up mine eyes unto the hills; from whence cometh my help?" It didn't matter then, nor has it since, that virtually everyone reads this Psalm to mean that our help comes from the hills. That understanding ignores the semi-colon after hills, and takes no account of the next line, "My help cometh from the Lord, who hast made heaven and earth." OH nor Jeff could have cared less what the verse meant. Its content was irrelevant.It had the cadence, the gravitas for which they were both desperately looking.

Later OH, would often would write and speak of this event. (He was called on to do this in the ordination screening in a latter day replication of the Massachusetts Bay Colony elders' requirement that one describe his conversion experience before he could have a piece of the action.) He thought he and Jeff must have been in the church praying and reading for about an hour, before, exhausted, he suggested they head back to the dorm.

"I can't believe what happened in there," Jeff said on their walk back. It took them considerably longer to get home because neither had paid attention to their route. "I don't think I've ever felt so calm, so totally at peace in myself. What do you think happened in there?"

"I have no idea," Our Hero answered, "but whatever it was, I think it was about the most powerful thing I have ever been through."

"Me, too."

They walked the rest of the way in silence except for an occasional exchange when they reached a corner, about which way to turn. When they finally found their way back to the quadrangle, Jeff turned to him. OH would say later that in the dim light of that quadrangle, the only light a low wattage bulb in a lantern several yards away, Jeff's face shown with a bright white. Like an angel.

"Thanks," Jeff said, "I feel like you saved my life."

"You're welcome, but it didn't feel to me like I did anything. Whatever happened, I didn't do it. It feels like whatever it was, it saved my life, too."

The two sobered boys parted. In the morning when OH staggered sleepily out of his room for his 8am class, having had time only to splash water on his face, Jeff was waiting outside his door.

"Morning."

Jeff ignored his greeting. "Look, I have no idea what happened last night, but I've been up most of the night thinking about it." OH nodded to let him know it had been like that for him, too. "I'm going to forget it ever happened, OK? I mean it was too weird. And I'd really appreciate it if you didn't say anything about it to any of our friends, OK?"

"Sure, fine. But I don't think I can forget about it. It feels like the most important thing that's ever happened to me and I think it might have changed my whole life."

It did change his life. Or it became the story that he told to try to explain to anyone who asked how he happened to go to seminary and get ordained. Was it the real reason? He'd likely still tell you it was, even though he now would try to describe and explain it, even without irony, in ways that required no supernatural explanation. Fact is, nearly a half century later, he still hasn't sorted it out. Even knowing that Freud would diagnose it as hysteria, he doesn't.

STIGMATA

A Riff On OH's Preoccupation With The Nature Of Spiritual Knowledge And Power As It Compares With Worldly Knowledge And Power

But what about this?

That incident freshman year set in motion the elaborate, not terribly demanding, but lengthy, process that led OH from having a vague notion of being an ordained person, to the moment when the Bishop lay hands on your head in the climax to an ancient mysterious passage.

In the course of that process, OH went to the seminary to be interviewed for admission. He felt excited and nervous, not sure what to expect. The seminary was in Cambridge, Massachusetts and though he sensed the school was eager to be accepted in the hard headed academic life of that over-brained city. He also thought it possible that he would need to persuade someone of the authenticity of his "call". It was, after all, Massachusetts.

It was a bitter cold January morning. An icy rain the night before had made the roads and sidewalks treacherous. He parked his powder-blue Nash Rambler next to a snow bank and as he stepped out of the car, his feet went out from under him and he fell forward. OH reached out to brace himself and the palms of both hands were punctured by ice shards as he went down. He hadn't time, nor did he know where to go to clean himself up, so he walked into the Dean's office where he was greeted by the Dean's secretary.

"May I help you?" she asked with a cheery smile.

"I'm here for an interview with the Dean." Without thinking about what he was about to do, he held out his hands and showed the attractive woman his bleeding palms. She studied him for a moment, then said, "You show me your side and your feet, and if they're bleeding, you get in without any interview."

They both laughed. OH felt exhilarated, though it would be decades before he could explain exactly why. She directed him to the bathroom where he, reluctantly, washed and wiped his hands free of blood. When he came out, studying his hands that were still oozing, the Dean, a handsome silver-haired dignitary in creased gray suit and vest, his movie-star handsome face set off by his linen-white clerical collar, was standing talking with his secretary.

"Here he is now," she said. "How's your stigmata?"

Self-conscious and only vaguely aware of what "stigmata" meant, he held out his hands, palms up.

"Young man," the Dean addressed him in a stained glass voice that he would forever associate with the voice of God, "at this seminary we frown on hysterical displays of piety."

For the next 30 years he would wrestle with powerful impulses, sometimes bordering on convictions. He knew they were emotional, some would say hysterical, and were so conflicting, wrenching him between his rational and non-rational dimensions that they sometimes made him feel like a schizophrenic. Though he never actually heard voices, sometimes he wondered if he was being addressed subliminally. By his own unconscious or by God, he couldn't say. Nor could be say what distinguished one from the other.

One was an updated version of the Covenant requirement of the old Massachusetts Bay Colony, at least for the ordained. From the outset it was clear there were people among his seminary classmates who, though they would understand and describe it differently from each other, felt called by God to that work. And there were others for whom it was a choice much like a choice for law or medical school, made with a sober eye on working conditions and opportunities.

Our Hero initially regarded the second group as fraudulent, a religious version of Holden Caulfield's "phonies." When he examined it carefully, which he seldom did, he realized that he felt the same sacred requirement ought to be part of the test for becoming a doctor. But not a lawyer. A sacred calling, priest, doctor, teacher, required a more solemn charge than a mere job or other profession. Separate from the pack.

The opposite pull grew stronger in him as he practiced parish ministry and entered into more and deeper psychotherapy. The therapist with whom he worked during his first years as a parish rector, when OH was in his early 30s, persuaded him that a person can only really have contempt for himself. He can project that contempt onto others, but it is a piece of himself that has triggered it. This insight caused him both to question his lack of respect for several of his more hard-headed colleagues, whom he decided may have been more mature and self-insightful than he in facing their own motives, and his own sense of having been called by God.

Maybe it didn't matter. And if you insist on talking about God and being called, who's to say that can't all be worked out in a rational consideration of the daily details of the work, just as well, maybe with more honesty, as it can in a rush of adrenaline in a late adolescent male-bonding moment?

Or a spontaneous opening of a wound in hands, feet or side?

Our Hero carries in his shame bank of memory his phony posing as a fully formed mystic, shortly after his college conversion experience. And in precisely the setting that would one day represent the dimension he (oh how he hated to admit it) held in contempt; middle-American protestant piety.

He was courting a college co-ed classmate from nearby suburban Connecticut. Her father, heir to a seat on the New York Stock Exchange, was a Deacon in the Lutheran Church in their town. Weekends when Our Hero visited with his girlfriend, church was always on their agenda. He secretly made fun of the mealy mouthed piety of the pastor. And OH posed as a spiritual guru. He was in fact intimidated by the vast wealth and power of his girlfriend's family, which he regarded as ill-gotten. He still believed power and influence rightfully belonged to the intellectual elite. And this family's intellectual life was informed solely by the Reader's Digest. He hoped they might fall for his posing as a spiritual guru, might think he held some secret power they knew nothing about. In fact he hoped he might actually gain esoteric knowledge someday. He hated feeling at a disadvantage, not only naked in the men's locker room, but in the presence of anyone who had reached a high station or made a lot of money. Might spiritual fine-tuning prove a match for worldly power?

And though he never felt it worked, he became aware that powerful people, especially businessmen, handled their exchanges with him gingerly, as if he possessed some pipeline to power they didn't. So was that, he wondered, after several decades of servicing the shapeless desires of churchgoers, the real function of church? To arouse the hunger and fear in people, to stir their curiosity about and envy of a dimension they felt they lacked. A dimension perhaps the ordained had? A sort of transactional stigmata?

Two images came to dominate his thinking. The first was inoculation. Going to church, he thought, was like getting vaccinated against polio or smallpox. The vaccine is made of a small amount of the dreaded disease that has been treated, titrated, filtered through membranes, monkey's kidney tissue, so that it tricks the immune system into sensing that the body has been exposed to the disease. The immune system manufactures antibodies that protect the person should he ever encounter a full attack of the disease. It is a brilliant strategy that has rid the world of several plagues that threatened to extinct our species.

By carefully organizing and managing a seeming encounter with the ineffable God, the church provides the worshipper with a vague spiritual whiff without the threat of being overpowered by a meeting with the Wholly Other.

The other image was of unintended risk. Occasionally a batch of the vaccine becomes more potent than intended and the inoculation is lethal rather than protective. Martin Luther was probably a perfectly ordinary young monk when he joined the Augustinian Order. The odds were that he would live out his days in the obscurity of the cloister. But his brush with the holy so infected and inflamed him that he became a carrier of life-changing trouble that infected and rearranged the entire western world.

Our Hero considered all that on a mission he and several of his classmates took to Washington, D.C. in 1964 when the Public Accommodations Bill of the Civil Rights Bill was languishing in a Senate filibuster. A student at Jewish Theological Seminary in New York organized a schedule for Protestant, Roman Catholic and Jewish seminarians to come to Washington and stand a 24-hour vigil at the Lincoln Memorial until the bill was voted up or down. The students from Our Hero's seminary slept on air mattresses in the basement of an Augustinian monastery in NE Washington.

The first night, at dinner, one of the monks told them about their worship service two weeks earlier in which they had sung, for the first time, Luther's hymn, "A Mighty Fortress Is Our God."

"Seemed like a pretty progressive, if not radical move for us," the young monk explained, "because the whole idea of hymn singing is pretty new to us, introduced since Vatican II. And then this hymn was written by our once colleague, then betrayer, Martin Luther."

"How did it go?"

"We were singing along pretty well; it's a fun, full-bodied song, when all of a sudden, the corpus on the crucifix, a twice life-sized bronze of Jesus, maybe because of the unaccustomed strong vibrations from our usually timid organ, came loose from its fastenings, fell off the cross and bounced across the stone chancel floor, clattering loudly, startling everyone. It came to rest face-down against the altar."

"Holy Shit," Our Hero exclaimed, "what did you guys do?"

"We kept on singing, watched the Prior to see what he would do, until the organist got to laughing so hard he couldn't keep playing. And the whole place cracked up."

Maybe, dear reader, you can see how Our Hero's expectations and hopes got raised in those notorious 60s, hopes that the whole world was being made new. Maybe religion, along with politics, was about to take a daring turn. Who would have predicted that Pope John XXIII would so unnerve his fellow Cardinals that they would elect as his successor someone who not only would stuff all that humor and experimental religion back into the closet, but having come from an eastern European nation where he had been weaned on totalitarianism, would spend his long rein seeing to the tightening down of the ecclesiastical screws?

As this is being written, OH is contemplating the conclave begun this very morning in the Sistine Chapel in Vatican City where the College of Cardinals has convened to choose a successor to John Paul II. After scanning the list of possibilities in the New York Times, OH has no preference. What he hopes is that, as happened when John XXIII was chosen, the new Pope will surprise his colleagues and swing the doors of the church open, at least a little. But he doubts that will happen.

[His doubts were hardly strong enough to have imagined the election of the German cardinal, Ratzinger, the prelate most associated with the hard line. They should have been.]

Here's a question that rolls around in OH as he considers the turns of history he has seen; will he, before he dies, see the pendulum swing back from the conservative, bottom-line mentality that has dominated western culture the past thirty years? Will his children? Or grandchildren?

ORGANIZED RELIGION AS SELF-DIDDLING

The other image Our Hero found useful in describing church religion was masturbation. He drew this analogy: church is to God as masturbation is to sexual intercourse.

Now don't misunderstand; he did not mean to diminish the significance of masturbation, or to suggest that it is a counterfeit expression of sex. He had long subscribed to the notion that masturbation is one legitimate choice among many, a happy way to experience the delight of orgasm without the messiness of the encounter with another naked person.

But it is different.

And, just as it is possible that pleasuring one's self may prove an incentive for venturing into the more complex arena of sexual encounter with another, so church-going could, conceivably, stimulate a worshipper's appetite for the richer, more dangerous experience. But most people, being people, will settle.

And that, Our Hero decided, is probably a good thing. What if all those who watched Martha Stewart on television or read her magazine, determined to actually live out her suggestions? The world would quickly descend into a chaos that would make the planet ever more inhospitable. Most of us are spectators, satisfied to watch the super-stars move more than their share of volume of atoms and molecules. If it were otherwise, if more of us were more active, less passive, we would have already depleted the planet's resources.

THE LEATHER BAR
A STUDY IN SHAME & GRACE

The time is the beginning of fall term of Our Hero's sophomore year in college. In those days before college credit cards or internet, one paid one's bills in this way; a hand drawn check. Tuition was $3000, and Our Hero carried a check made out by his father to The University of Pennsylvania for $1500 for the first half year.

When he finally got to the front of the line, the person at the desk told him the first semester's tuition was $1300. After some deliberations involving higher ups than the table-man, it was agreed that the University would give Our Hero $200 in cash, a sum larger by a factor of four than he had previously managed. Four $50 bills which he carefully placed in the second pocket of his wallet.

The large wad felt to him like a branding, imprinting itself on his rear end, and he was eager to refund the money to his father (though he failed to mention it in his weekly phone call home), which he planned to do when he went to Boston for the Penn-Harvard football game three weeks hence.

He hooked a ride with friends on the Friday and was dropped off on Washington Street in Wellesley where he was to call his mother to pick him up. He looked around for a phone booth. He was standing in front of W.W. Winship, a leather store that had sold fine leather goods to Boston moguls for three generations.

His eye was caught immediately by a tan leather portable bar, displayed standing open in Winship's window, so you saw the green leather interior and the bone-handled shot glass. Our Hero felt his pulse quicken. Imagine showing up at a football game with such a thing stocked with a bottle of gin and one of bourbon. For him it was as unimaginable and unattainable as the blue MG of his friend who had driven him from Philadelphia.

He crossed the street to use the phone booth and call his mother, who greeted him excitedly and said she would be along in about 20 minutes.

He crossed back over the street and walked back and forth trying to appear as if he was merely walking, not riveted by that leather bar. On an impulse that, considering it years later, seemed totally involuntary, OH went through Winship's door and walked to the display to look at it without the distortion of the window glass.

"May I help you?" He hadn't seen the salesman, dressed in Brooks Brothers tweeds, but he understood the question's tone to mean that the man knew from OH's college appearance that he didn't carry the financial heft of a Winship customer.

"Oh, no, thank you," he knew how flustered he sounded, wishing he had the savoir faire of his rich friends. "I was just looking at that leather bar in the window."

"Handsome, isn't it?" The tweed man leaned across and lifted the bar from the window and placed it on a table in the middle of the room. Our Hero mentally calculated how long it would be before his mother showed up. She was usually late, drove slowly—a good thing since she always had a sherry before lunch.

"How much is it?" Our Hero mentally winced, knowing he was moving way too fast. Small talk and appearing to feel comfortable, casual when his nervous system was in high rev had never worked for him.

The salesman looked to deliver his coup de grace; "One-hundred-and eighty dollars," he solemnly pronounced, "with three gold embossed initials, exactly Two-hundred dollars."

The rest remains a blur in Our Hero's mind. What he knows is that he bought it, handed over the two-hundred dollars that had been causing the unfamiliar bulge in his wallet, revealed his initials to the snotty salesman, and exited the store just in time to flag down his mother who was cruising by in her bronze Chevy Impala.

The following week, after he picked up his new leather bar with his initials handsomely embossed in gilt, was nerve-wracking for Our Hero. He waited until both his parents were out of the house, difficult since his mother only went out a couple of times a month—this time to get her hair washed and set. He offered to drive her and pick her up, an errand of mercy for an agoraphobic. He put the bar, still in its cardboard box, in the back of his closet, covered it with a blanket, and used every ounce of mental energy not required for sustaining his life that week, for trying to figure out how he was going to get the bar out of the house without his father knowing about it.

On Wednesday, having been to a Red Sox game in Fenway Park, the coldest place on earth in April, Our Hero came home just as the sun was setting, happy to be indoors with some hope of getting warm. As he walked in the house he saw through the door only the right elbow and shoulder of his father sitting in the den in a chair, not his usual place to light after a day's work. Our Hero's stomach tightened. He hadn't clicked the front door shut behind him before he heard his father's voice.

"Could you come in here for a moment, Son?"

As he stepped his first halting step into the room he saw the bar on the floor next to his father's chair, still in its cardboard box. "Have a seat," his father commanded, motioning to the tiger maple desk-chair he had obviously placed opposite him for this purpose. There was a wet ring around the base of the highball glass on the arm of his father's chair, the glass one-third full of dark brown bourbon. Our Hero sensed that either his father had been sitting waiting for close to an hour or was drinking faster than his usual pace. Neither possibility reassured Our Hero.

"What's this?" his father motioned to the box on the floor.

"A portable bar."

"Whose is it?"

"Mine."

"Where'd you get it?"

"Winship's."

"You bought a leather bar from W.W. Winship?"

"Yes, sir."

"How much did it cost?"

"$Two-hundred dollars. With three initials."

"You paid $200 for a leather bar and put your initials on it?"

"Yes, sir."

Our Hero wondered for years how long the pause was before his father spoke. He figured he probably exaggerated it in his memory because of his anxiety. Still, he would believe it was minutes long. Long enough for him to wonder if he was going to be able to stay sitting there without his bowels betraying him. His father stared at him and he didn't dare take his eyes off his father. They sat stock still considering each other like two gunslingers facing off. Finally his father looked down at his feet, all the air seemed to go out of him. He looked small, defeated. Our Hero tried to will his father to yell at him, swear, shake his fist. But he knew he wasn't going to do that.

"I can't find the words to tell you how disappointed I am in you," his father said. He stood up from his chair, paused, reached down for his glass, picked it up and walked into the kitchen. Our Hero could hear him fill the glass with ice, then the sound of pouring bourbon. He heard his father's footsteps going down the hall to the living room on the other side of the house. OH supposed he would have taken his usual chair by the TV.

After another period of indeterminate length during which he sat in the hardback chair looking at the box opposite him, wondering what he was going to do next, he got up, picked the box up, went to his room and put the bar back in his closet. They never spoke about it again.

Twenty years later, having been Rector of a parish in suburban Boston for seven years, Our Hero found himself in conflict with his Vestry, the lay governing body of the church. The issues were slippery, unclear, having to do with the way he communicated with the church about money and Jesus. Several of the men challenged his judgment, even suggested he might be playing fast and loose with his mystic authority, trying to keep parishioners in the dark so he could operate without opposition. It took OH back to the days when he hoped to intimidate his girlfriend's family with his phony spiritual insight.

"They don't buy it," he told himself. They may not have understood his spiritual talk, but they weren't stupid about power and they knew when they were being manipulated.

During the meetings, when the conflict came up, what troubled Our Hero most was his sense of shame. Sometimes he felt as if those who were angry at him, though he could come up with reasonable answers to their objections, might be justified. Maybe he was devious. Not perfect.

Time, he decided, to find himself a therapist before he betrayed himself and fucked up the rest of his career. Not to mention his life.

The therapist quickly picked up on what was up with his paralysis during the meetings.

"You sound like you're overwhelmed with shame," he observed. "Can you tell me a time in your life when you felt especially ashamed?"

Immediately Our Hero remembered the incident with his father and the leather bar. The therapist seemed fascinated, leaned forward in his chair, asked an occasional leading question as the story unfolded in lurid detail. When he finished telling, the therapist asked him, "Do you still have that bar?" Our Hero told him that he did and knew exactly where it was, even though in the 20 years since he had bought it he had used it only once. The therapist asked him, "Would you bring it with you to our next meeting? I'd really like to see it."

He did bring it, feeling awkward as he handed it to the therapist. The therapist turned it around in his hands several times, opened it, running his fingers over the still supple leather, ending up tracing the gold initials with his forefinger.

"Nice," he said, "high grade leather. I used to raise cattle and this is the real stuff." They sat for a moment in silence. Our Hero relived the long silence with his father twenty years earlier.

"Tell you what," the therapist said, "let's replay that scene when you came home and your father had the bar by his chair. You're going to play yourself and I'm going to play your father. OK? Let's go."

And they did. Our Hero was amazed that the therapist remembered his father's part verbatim, even got the inflection right when he said, "$200? You paid $200 for a leather bar?"

"Uh huh," Our Hero answered obediently. This time a much longer silence during which Our Hero felt light headed; his stomach lurched a couple of times. Finally the therapist spoke.

"You hot shit! You had $200 burning a hole in your pocket and you bought this gorgeous leather bar! You are the best! I'm so proud of you I could burst."

Our Hero looked at his therapist in disbelief. He felt cautious. He was certain he was being set up.

"All my life I've wanted to do something outrageous, something fun and over the top, but I never had the balls. I always had to play it straight, never dared step outside the line and make a scary choice for myself. But you've done it. My son, my own flesh and blood has balls, imagination. God, I am so happy to have you for a son. You're everything I've always wanted to be myself."

Our Hero began to cry, softly. "You mean . . . ?"

"Look," the therapist was still speaking in the voice he had adopted to play his father, "I've always loved you. But right now, knowing you have the energy to do something so life-giving, I feel like I'm about to come apart I'm so proud of you. You'll never know how many times I've dreamed of doing something like this, only to give it up as too risky."

Another decade passed and Our Hero, rummaging through his closet one day in search of tax records from the previous year, pulled back an old blanket and uncovered the leather bar. He pulled it out, brushed off the dust and opened it. He was pleased that it felt and looked just as it had the day he took it from Winship's.

"Damn," he thought, this is what I have been trying to get across in my preaching for so long I had almost forgotten about it. The Gospel reading for the following Sunday was the story of the Prodigal Son in which the son asks for his inheritance and then goes off and squanders it. He comes back abjectly, defeated, ashamed, and begs his father to take him back, only not as a son but as a servant taking care of the pigs. The father hardly seems to hear his wayward son's apologies. He embraces him, weeps for joy at his return and holds a huge feast to celebrate.

The Bible story, though it outraged a couple of people in the congregation every time it came up, was Our Hero's favorite. Now, looking at the bar, he relived the story from his own life.

So he took the bar into church the next Sunday and, at the sermon time, carried it the length of the long aisle as he told the story, translating into the idiom of his experience with the bar, his father and the therapist.

Two families left the church that day because they felt Our Hero lacked the dignity appropriate to proper church and preacher.

OH tried not to appear smug, In fact he had to agree with them.

Though Our Hero and his father didn't speak of the bar matter again during the remaining 28 years of his father's life, they did speak about another long buried matter just two weeks before his father died. He died, by the way, with such easy willingness, no resistance to slipping into eternity, that Our Hero very nearly relaxed about it himself.

Gertrude; Shame & Grace II

His father was in bed full time, lung cancer. He got up, with help, only to go to the toilet. His head was clear most of the time, happily maintained on the morphine perfectly titrated by the hospice worker who, though she lacked formal medical training and had only an eighth grade education, came from the bowels of Baltimore's ghetto where she learned more about drugs than you can learn at any medical school.

Our Hero was talking with his father late one night, when everyone else in the house was asleep. They were talking about these remarkable women who were caring for him. Two of them were now working 12 hour shifts, and had been for 10 days. The night woman was downstairs taking a break while OH and his father talked.

"That Grace is quite a gal," his father said, a wide smile spreading across his face which was sunburned red from the fever he was running. "You know, having been raised in the south, I never figured I'd come to the point at which I was totally dependent on a black woman. You just never know, do you?"

A powerful and distinct memory flooded OH at that moment. About a time in the town in North Carolina where their family lived when he was a boy. His father was putting him to bed. Bedtime was his favorite because, when his father was home, he would put Our Hero to bed and, between his father's fatigue from a day of working and the two or three highballs of bourbon he always drank in the evening, he was gentle and mellow, unguarded.

"Dad," he asked his now dying father, whose sunken face looked like the face of the dying Jesus, "do you remember the night you were putting me to bed, and after you had read to me, you stopped and looked down at me with a serious expression and said to me; "Son, I heard you call

Gertrude 'Mam' tonight when she passed the potatoes to you. I know you love Gertie; we all do. But, Son, you just musn't call a negro 'Mam.' It confuses and embarrasses them. It's disrespectful of your Mom and of Gertrude."

"I remember feeling ashamed for not knowing, for breaking a taboo, and I remember promising not to do it again. Which I probably didn't, for years. Sure marks the passage of time, doesn't it?"

The color in his father's face became even more florid. "I never said that to you," he protested with more energy than OH had heard in his voice in days.

Our Hero was about to insist that of course he had; it certainly wasn't something he could have invented (was it?), when Grace, the night nurse, walked into the room.

"What you two boys talkin' about?" she asked, laughing.

His father died five days later, quietly, so quietly it made OH queasy when he helped load his body into the green bag the undertaker brought to the house. "What if he's not really quite dead? What if he wakes up in there?" he couldn't stop his mind from asking.

At the burial he looked across the open grave to where Grace stood. He wondered whether racism gets cleared up when you die. A friend of OH's had married a black woman, another a Laotian; both, he knew, in part to try to banish their racism. He knew because he understood that's what he would like to do. So, in separate conversations, he asked them, "Did it work?"

"No," the one who married an American black said. "I grew just as restless in my marriage to her as I had to Marian." Marian was his first wife, a perfect match, except she bored him. Which is to say she showed him more of himself than he cared to see.

The other friend, the one who married a Laotian, from Laos' northern provinces, said it had worked pretty well for him. "I really got so I could look at her and not see her darker complexion and slanted eyes. But then a funny thing happened. Her family came to this country. I got them visas, even got her brother a green card, and they came to live here. It fucked up our marriage something awful. You know why? They were racists. They hated white westerners, thought we were pigs, their social and intellectual inferiors. I've had a lot of people hate me for all sorts of reasons," he said, "but being held in contempt for my ethnic origins was a brand new experience."

"How did you manage to stay married?"

"I told Chin I wasn't going to have any more to do with them. I said she'd have to choose."

"Did she?"

"Kind of. They left one day without telling either of us. They went back to Laos. Called us when they were back in home and said they wanted to live in Laos. Chin was devastated. But she's a practical woman and she had no interest in leaving her life here. But I know she also still holds me in contempt. Always will. Same reason as her family. Wrong race, don't measure up."

"Sounds like a lot of marriages."

Our Hero admitted one day to his children that when he met someone of another race, that was the first thing he noticed about them. "It takes me some time to figure out whether that is going to be the only thing about them that counts with me. I'm never sure if I will get by that so I can meet the person."

They were shocked. "You're shitting me."

Good/Bad . . . Right/Wrong
Reality Cannot Be Crippled

Our Hero spends some part of every week studying the ocean. Standing, looking at it for up to a couple of hours, wondering how one might portray, whether in words or image, still or moving, what is clearly forever in motion.

"You do understand," he said to his daughter one afternoon as the two of them sat in low chairs on the beach, their feet dug into warm sand while a cool breeze fanned their faces, "that the ocean is just like your arm, or for that matter, the chair you're sitting on?"

"You mean because it's water, like us?" She was pretty sharp for a 12 year old, "Or because it is always moving, every bit of it?"

"Yes," he answered.

If you miss this, you will miss the organizing principle of Our Hero's existence, which is that there can be no organizing principle. Because nothing stands still long enough to plant that fulcrum from which Archimedes claimed he could move the earth. Whether that consigns OH to hopeless chaos or opens a new, creative dimension of reality, will depend on a number of things waiting to be revealed. One of you will find this vision depressing and paralyzing, while another will feel a surge of new energy at such a daring penetration of imagination breaking apart old structures. Both responses are legitimate. And accurate.

So one afternoon as he stood on the promenade by the beach considering the ocean, he was startled to see a wheelchair getting knocked around in the edge of the surf. Being a Good Samaritan by training he rushed down and grabbed hold of the chair. It was sunk deep into the soft sand. He tugged to free it so he could pull it safely up above the tide line.

"Leave the fucking chair where it is!" The voice was clear even above the roar of the surf. He looked around but couldn't tell who had yelled at him. "Over here." Looking in the direction the voice came from, he could see just the top of a man's head above the sea wall. He walked up from the water's edge and pulled himself over the wall where a man was lying on a tricycle, his head at one end and his feet at the other, on pedals. The handle bars were high above his head like a modified Harley.

"Makes you wonder, huh?" The man smiled at him. He studied the man and his bike for a moment. His kids had been at him for years for the way he stared at people. The man lying on his bicycle seemed comfortable waiting for him to complete his exam.

"Nice bike, man."

"Thanks. It's especially nice if your lower body has checked out."

"Paraplegic, huh? How'd it happen?"

"Tumor on my spine. Surgeon geniuses figured out a way to remove the tumor, but slipped ever so slightly." He laughed a belly laugh. "Don't look so whacked out, man; I've figured out how to make this into one amazing adventure. Probably at least as rich as yours."

"OK, I'll buy that. What about that wheel chair bouncing around in the surf?"

"That's Jack's. He's out there swimming those buoys. That's his van parked there on the beach. He'll need the chair to get him back in the van when he comes in. We swim here a lot. Training for a triathlon we're doing in August."

It was the beginning of a chapter that was to change Our Hero's picture of his life. Jim was the guy on his back on the tricycle, and he and Jack became OH's cyber companions and sometime swimming buddies. Like his dog, who regarded most matters according to whether they could be eaten, licked, peed on or mounted, the two paraplegic men introduced Our Hero to a new way of considering his world.

Especially of considering any matters having to do with right and wrong, or good and bad. Our Hero, in his priestly days, had thought he was pretty evolved in these matters, having absorbed the Jungian understanding of the psyche's light and shadow. But he was to discover that having one's body rearranged in such a way as to cause one to take an entirely new tack in making one's way in the world, caused, at least in these two new friends, a perspective far more radical than he had considered before. And being buoyant in the ocean with them caused OH to resonate with them in ways that thrilled him and further isolated him from the four-limbed mainstream from which he had come.

The Dalai Lama, whom OH much admired and thought hopelessly out of touch with reality, in much the way all the religious leaders he had known were out of touch, wrote an article in which he described experiments he had seen at the University of Minnesota. The experiments tried to measure activity in the mind, ("or brain as you in the west call it" . . . this aside required more quiet wondering by Our Hero) while people were sitting in meditation.

A brain scan showed a small area on the left side and one on the right, each side glowing with active energy depending on whether the subject was experiencing tranquility, compassion, or anxiety, competition. An order of Roman Catholic Nuns and some Zen Monks, considered proficient at entering altered states, showed consistently more activity on the left, compassion side when they were sitting meditating on compassion.

Though he didn't really understand the article, it impressed Our Hero and caused him to reconsider, for the thousandth time, regulary setting aside time to sit. And he wrote to his two paralyzed friends asking what they thought.

"The Dalai Lama is stuck in the old model of right and wrong, good and bad," Jim responded. "Why is it better to have compassion than to be angry or anxious? It depends on what's going on. These emotions and their commensurate activities have been hot wired into us because they have been useful, appropriate to situations we have faced that require us to make creative responses to what is happening. Love is not always a better response than hate and I would gladly challenge Jesus if he stood before me and made such a claim. But he likely wouldn't."

Our Hero's mind traveled back in time to a tense confrontation with an old Brit. Our Hero had preached a sermon pointing out that Jesus' telling the story in which the Samaritan figured as the hero, was offensive to the people who heard him. To righteous Jews, a Samaritan was scum, less than human. It would be to us if someone told us a story in which the guy who did the good deed while all the admirable types, clergy, sports heroes, rock stars, even successful business tycoons, let the wounded person just lie there, and the guy who helped him was Timothy McVey.

You may not remember Timothy McVey. He's been dead a couple of years. But at the time everyone knew who he was, because he had just been accused of blowing up the Federal Building in Oklahoma City in which lots of people, including children in a day care center, had been killed.

"So," OH had concluded the sermon, "if you want to understand how Jesus got himself killed, imagine him telling that story about the wounded man, and the only one who would help him turning out to be the Oklahoma City bomber. We would change the name of the story from The Good Samaritan to The Parable of The Good Oklahoma City Bomber."

It had, understandably, outraged some people, which had been OH's purpose, since he reckoned the story as Jesus told it would have outraged his hearers. What OH may not have fully considered, and wondered later if Jesus had, was the heat he was going to take for hitting people's hot spot. The beloved retired British priest often appointed himself a spokesman for the congregation.

"Couldn't you just once say out loud from the pulpit," the old Limey priest implored, "that you believe in the Ten Commandments? It would be very comforting to some people who are wondering if you have any morals."

"But we're talking the new dispensation," Our Hero tried to sound calm, "in which Jesus says the commandments are not written on stone but in our hearts."

"Well then," the old cleric pressed on pointlessly, "could you just say you believe in one of the 10?"

When OH pointed to Jesus' radical rejection of the Law, the learned Englishman looked disgusted. He suggested that Our Hero, was stuck in the 60s dispensation, promoting easy feel-good emotion over serious ethical engagement. Our Hero felt deflated. Perhaps he should remain in his old idiom—mainstream American religion—where he could consider himself merely groovy-60s harmless, and remain unchallenged, keeping his sometimes offensive views under wraps. Truth was, he knew, the Englishman had a point.

THE DIVING DENTIST AND THE OLYMPIC SAILOR DYING ON HOLIDAY

"Could you come over this afternoon?" The question was routine, asked of OH endlessly. Twice in a space of a few years, it was different. But both times it sounded so lacking in urgency, that even the second time, it didn't occur to Our Hero to tighten his sphincter as he normally did when recognizing a moment that would plunge him into the depths. A seemingly simple moment that would squeeze all the air from his lungs. And cause him to wonder whether his preaching was mere posturing. His wife was the only one who dared suggest that, for all his apparent intimacy with death, he would likely be terrified when his own time came.

In the first instance it was the wife of a well-known and even beloved dentist, beloved for his sense of adventure, not his unpleasant probing of people's mouths. She had just been notified of a change in her status, from wife to widow, by her husband's diving friends who found her husband's body caught in the kelp a couple of hundred yards offshore.

The second, another wife, also suddenly changed by a phone call, telling her that her husband, world class sailor, while skippering a prototype boat in San Francisco Bay, the hiking-out platform broke and the entire crew had fallen into the icy waters. He saw to the well-being of his crew, and was then pulled, lifeless, into the rescue boat.

In one sense routine. We humans, though we decided some time ago to try our hand on land, cannot seem to stay away from the water in which we can no longer draw a good breath. Drowning, some say, is one of the preferred deaths, the replacement of 0_2 with H_20 causing a release of endorphins into the brain, quickly turns the struggle into a euphoric surrender. Though it has always seemed presumptuous of those of us who have yet to drown to speak descriptively of the experience, rather like the dubious near-death experiences (you did say "near" death?) that entertain us at the check-out counter. Our Hero has long taken comfort in the idea, when not challenged by his firmly grounded wife, imagining that he might, when the time comes (when does the time come?), swim away from shore.

What fascinated Our Hero about the two phone calls was their tone. No hysteria. Had he not asked, he thought the two women might not have told him the reason they wanted him to come by. How much that had to do with the old Catholic notion of calling the priest immediately after calling the undertaker, a task assigned by the circumstance, to be done without great affect, and how much to the personalities of the two women, he was never certain.

Our Hero always got a rush from these moments, a shot of adrenaline he assumed was programmed into him to provide the courage and imagination he would need in the ensuing hours and days when he would become the coordinator of a drama with many parts. And many players.

And from the first death he tended as a 26 year old curate, the suicide of the Junior high principal in a Midwestern town who had no wish to engage in the sordid search for the culprit who had drained the band uniform bank account, Our Hero understood that the priest was the only one with a perspective from which he could see all the parts at once. He became like the prompter in the play, knowing everyone's part and sometimes needing to whisper a prompt when someone was distracted and missed their lines. Only, oddly, in this drama, he also—at strategic moments—took center stage for a moment.

Neither man, as it turned out, had drowned. The dentist had air left in his tank. The sailor had no water in his lungs. He had died before he went face down in the water.

In both cases the families responded dutifully to the requests of the many actors in the drama, agreeing to have their husbands' bodies sliced into tiny slivers of cells that were sent to labs across the planet, searching for some explanation of how they had been changed from alive to dead. The women were clear that the cause of their husband's deaths made no real difference to them, since it would have no bearing on their or their husbands' status. Both were clear that anything short of returning their husband to life was of little interest to them. But both were realists, understanding the ways of the world and didn't interfere with the anxious doctors' wish to name the cause of death.

Well, nothing ever turned up. Nothing. No scar tissue on either heart muscle, no toxins in their body fluids. Every attempt to grow something lethal in their cells came to naught. Our Hero wondered what percent of their bodies had been available to be cremated after the various labs had taken their tissues.

"I knew they weren't going to find anything," the sailor's widow told Our Hero one afternoon when he dropped by on a pastoral call. "He died. End of story. What imaginable difference do they think it would make to give his death a name more medically esoteric than dead?"

"I knew he would die like that," the dentist's widow said to him. "He knew it too. We even talked about it a few days before he died." She laughed. It had been a few months, but Our Hero nonetheless thought she was heroic to dare to laugh openly about it.

"You know he was a total Albert Schweitzer, an animal lover. He loved being out there in that kelp bed with the lobsters and sharks and all the weird organisms that hang out there. Liked it maybe better than being in a room full of people, even people he liked. If I had to come up with a reason he died out there, when there seems to have been nothing wrong with his body, I'd say it was because he chose it."

"Does that piss you off at all? I mean he left you with an awful lot of life by yourself. With more than a few details to tend to."

"No. He didn't owe me any more than he gave me. And I can't say I see what the big deal is about 20 or 30 more years. Life is what it is and then it's over. And I don't consider myself either alone or without him. It's damn different all right, and some things about that are pretty good and some pretty bad. But that's how it was when he came home at night too."

"You really loved him, didn't you?"

"Passionately, like a part of my own body. I miss his body the way I imagine I'd miss a limb."

The sailor's widow explained something to Our Hero that she apparently thought might need clearing up.

"You know he was Jewish, right?"

"Meaning?"

"Meaning he didn't believe in heaven."

"And do you?"

"No, well not at least the way I hear it talked about most of the time. It seems pointless, sort of adolescent, an ego storm that makes us need to believe the universe couldn't carry on without us."

"So what do you think happens?" Our Hero figured he must be getting pretty comfortable with this widow to ask her the questions he was used to being asked by the bereaved.

"Beats me. But whatever life is, and I sometimes feel like I have some vague idea about that, I think it is indelible. It's not clear to me whether we've always been a part of it or stumbled into it in this existence. But once having become a part of it, I suspect we're always part of it. This life business, once we opt for it, strikes me as somehow irrevocable."

"Sort of like the idea that matter is not created or destroyed, only transformed?"

"Yeah, same idea. But all the sentiment around it leaves me cold."

"Like your husband?"

OH was relieved when she laughed, a big belly laugh.

How come, Our Hero wondered, these two women showed so little outward affect toward their husbands' deaths? Oh they cried, and their bodies trembled visibly when they confronted the body. They experienced the exhaustion all grieving people seem to know. But there was none of the hysteria down the road he saw in so many, nor the depression or paralysis of will. Both women received the parade of mourners, thanked them, wrote their notes of gratitude, and moved on.

Our Hero wondered at first whether they may have had ice-cold marriages. But when he got to know the two widows he discovered the opposite was true. Something about their intimacy had made it possible for them to endure a heftier dose of reality than most people can. Intimacy and their husbands' affinity for the sea combined to make them open to and accepting of the risks of offering themselves. They always knew the inevitable outcome.

"My husband," the dentist's widow told OH one afternoon when he dropped by her house, "would leave a waiting room full of people when his friend called to say the visibility off Wind n' Sea Beach was suddenly prefect. He told me he was going to die in the ocean if he possibly could. At first I thought it was male bravado, but after a few years of seeing that look he had when he returned from an afternoon suspended beneath the surface, I knew he really meant it. I love the ocean, but I'm more land-based than he was. He really felt more alien, I think, walking on solid ground than he did suspended in salt water."

"Here's the deal about the ocean," thought Our Hero. It took him back to when he was a young boy, maybe fourth grade. He had learned that everything is made just like everything else—atoms, molecules, protons, neutrons. My body, this desk, the solar system. And what's more, the sense that anything is stationery is an illusion, because those atoms and molecules are always in motion. Always. Everything.

So what is it about the ocean that people can sit and look at it for hours on end? The ocean will not harbor the illusion, our dreams, of permanence. It changes colors, shapes, everything, constantly. Watching a fish make its way through water can trigger a mystic moment. Which is supporting which? When Our Hero was a boy, he went with his family on a ship from the west coast of the United States to the Philippines, a voyage of more than three weeks. As they entered Manila harbor, bronze boys in pongas paddled out to meet them. The boys were shouting something. A man standing on the top deck next to OH threw a coin into the water and a boy dove from his tiny boat. They could see him descend deep into the clear water, snatch the coin and turn and swim to the surface, where, beaming broadly, he held the coin up like the trophy Our Hero thought it truly was.

Alien on solid ground. An oxymoron, he knew. Nothing is solid, not really, and those diving boys woke in Our Hero a vestigial understanding that he was a visitor on the planet, not a permanent resident.

Remembering standing on that deck, reflecting on the times he had surrendered his body to the surge of currents and waves, Our Hero understood why the two widows were philosophical about their husbands' transformations. When it first occurs to you that you aren't here for long, your anxious ego will try to persuade you that is cause for despair, cosmic outrage. And you will derive great pleasure in staring down the ego. Because you will understand that it isn't cause for despair. For wonder, maybe. Despair, never.

The price of such a vision can be high. But such a pearl of wisdom! Nothing can match it for penetrating the dense mystery of our being here.

"But if the ocean is our symbol for reality," he realized, "then the mystery is moving, never still, and one person's sense of it is like a molecule of water, H_2O, salty, traveling at a yard a second as its wave comes ashore where it soaks the sand and, unless it is a molecule that marries the sand, returns to make another run. Endless."

GRUNION RUN IN THE EARTH'S ETHER

Come see the grunion run! The flyer came in the mail along with an ad for fresh watermelons just arrived at Von's Supermarket. OH never cared much for watermelons, because, well because they tasted like nothing but water, fresh water at that. But grunion, that was a different matter. Our Hero had assumed grunion were like snipes, a fiction invented long ago by horny young men who felt they needed to invent subterfuges to lure the objects of their desire to some venue that might cause them to want to merge their bodies as mightily as the young men desired. (Males must trick females into reproducing?) So when he saw the direct mailing from Scripps Aquarium he assumed it was some sort of joke, an attempt to break down his resistance so he would give money to the aquarium. And buy watermelons.

But it had a time and date and place so he decided to go. On the night the flyer advertised, he and his family and a few friends went to the beach, just steps from his house, under a full moon. It was a full two hours past his normal bedtime. The tide was full, perhaps even a flood tide. The local commercial interests, club, restaurants had turned off their floods so the only light was from the moon and from Our Hero's excitement at being so close to his ancestral home with several people who had claim to his passion. The six of them walked the beach for twenty minutes, running down with the backwash of each wave hoping to see some sign. Nothing. They were just about to decide their hopes were futile when Brian, husband of Our Hero's youngest daughter, cried, "There!" and ran at full sprint fifty yards north until he came to a lone grunion, the size and shape of your forefinger. She was balanced on her tail, spinning, wriggling, boring a hole in the wet sand, frantically rushing to finish her work before the next wave. Brian reached down to grab her

107

just as the wave came. That wave brought a hundred more grunion that each did their tail dance, burrowing into the sand. And now there were four hundred male grunion wrapping themselves around the females in an erotic apache dance. The next wave brought a thousand females and four thousand males.

Our Hero and his erotically challenged DNA were now immersed in a reprise of their own origins. Standing, running, exclaiming, beside themselves, chasing, quite literally, on the edge of their ancient home, their primordial instinct erotically charged, OH and his DNA did their ancient dance.

You would expect the thrill to subside, once the grunion—plentiful, predictable, wriggling, torn between their impulse to replicate themselves, the seeming universal immortality dream, and their survival instinct that spent their remaining energy after laying and fertilizing, to struggle back into the surf before they were stranded by the receding tide. A dilemma not faced by Burt Lancaster and Deborah Kerr in their famous edge of the surf scene. Over and over, wave after wave, hundreds of thousands, maybe millions of grunion, heroically risking everything.

The thrill did not subside. It grew as the numbers of grunion grew, until the wet sand between the high and low tide lines was covered with the performing fish. Our hero and his family, weary of chasing up and down the beach, finally simply stood, mesmerized. They felt they were watching a performance that would go on long after not only he and his youngest progeny were dead, but even after his species was gone from the earth. Primordial.

And he loved it.

SEEING SPOTS

Our hero's father had played good tennis until six months before he died of lung cancer. He more than made up in wile for what he lost in physical prowess. And the thrill of playing, and even more of winning, became more intense as he aged.

One day he approached the net, driving the ball deep into his opponent's backhand court, and when his opponent hit a weak, high return, our hero's father closed toward the net for an easy put-away. Instead the ball seemed to sail right through his racket strings, landing safely inside his own baseline. Twice more in the match the same thing happened.

The next morning he made an appointment with his eye doctor who examined him and told him he was a lucky man.

"You've had a stroke." the doctor explained, "A clot in a vessel in your eye has plugged up, stopping the flow of blood and you've lost a piece of your field of vision. You're lucky it was a tiny vessel in your eye and not a large one in your brain, or your heart. It will absorb and though you won't ever get that tiny piece of your field of vision back, you'll soon adjust so you'll never know it's there."

Though he started on a blood thinner, he experienced two more similar incidents. Lucky man—as the doctor had said—he continued to play good tennis, eventually not noticing the little holes in his field of vision. And—lucky man that he was—never had a debilitating stroke.

Instead he managed to grow a virile tumor in his lung and thus was able to exit this world, not in a pathetic, half paralyzed, mute state, but articulate right up to the end. His wife of 40 years departed in the same manner, though when she died they were no longer married. Amazing how the values they had imposed on each other all those years, prizing clever conversation, fearing the appearance of stupidity or weakness, even if caused by cancer, had prevailed on both their death beds. Each of them, when it became clear they would soon lose their ability to speak articulately and to move their bowels, turned face to the wall, and without so much as an extra vial of morphine, gave away a final breath without bothering to take another.

So when our hero began to see floaters in his field of vision, he wondered. When he checked it out, he was told it could be nothing, or, well, it could be the onrush of mortality. Flipping a coin was his way of working out which. The problem was that, given his age and his normal level of distraction, when he flipped the coin he couldn't remember whether heads was nothing to worry about and tails impending mortality. Or vice versa.

So he decided to pray about it, which is to say, turn it over to the gods.

Because, as he rounded 60 and headed for Social Security, Our Hero finally surrendered to a reality he had held off for all his younger years. Melancholy, always his casual companion, began to stalk him and he discovered exercise, not casual exercise, but strenuous, muscle-numbing exercise, was the only effective antidote. He knew that there were people, less gifted athletes than he, who loved athletics and exercise of any kind, and were never happier than when they were breathless and sweaty.

Perhaps because he feared failure above all else—well maybe humiliation almost as much—he never enjoyed doing anything in which he might be defeated. Or look stupid. Which, at least initially, and realistically, periodically forever, was inevitable. Who can pick up a golf club and, on first try, par the hole? So exercise was an effort. But in his declining years he embraced it with new enthusiasm since it turned out that if he exercised to the point of leg cramps and sore joints, his muscles jumping involuntarily—like gigged frog's legs—he didn't wake up the next morning choleric and anxious. But if he went more than 24 hours without exercise, only reading, thinking, wondering, which he prefers above all other use of oxygenated blood, and the day will become a blur of dark menacing emotions that make each step feel as if he were clearing a minefield.

Rationalism, the prejudice that action should be guided by reason, is a curse from which Our Hero struggled to be released as early as third grade. His Sunday School teacher found him one day, instead of cutting out saints from the heavy colored paper, and decorating an Easter—egg basket, writing blank verse poems. OH came upon one of those poems decades later and was surprised that—in third grade version—it anticipated one by John Updike which said that if a single one of the cells in Jesus' pre-resurrection body was missing from his post-resurrection body, then Easter was a farce.

[Reading the poem all those years later, OH thought it subtle wisdom, for a third-grader. He had less patience for 21st Century adults who held to the same literal demands of the Easter experience.]

He was used to being called back to task, but this teacher seemed delighted, and suggested that he ought to write more poems and she would collect them for his parents.

His parents?! I think not, he thought. But he did continue writing, and he had some pre-pubescent erotic thoughts about his teacher, his first inkling that sexual excitement would be tied to his passion for words and for any woman who would encourage his wondering. He filled a multi-page spiral bound book of construction paper with his wondering about God, Jesus and death. The book gathered dust in the attic over the years.

Fifty or more years later he came across several mentions, all in the space of a few days, of the bizarre issue of whether a severed head might have some momentary awareness after it has been separated from its body. During the French Revolution heads were rolling often because it was regarded as a more humane way to kill someone than hanging. Inevitably, some people became curious about whether the head might, even for an instant, retain some awareness.

You would be right in regarding this subject as morbid, but surely there is not a person alive (or maybe dead in the case of the guillotined), who, if they can get past their squeamishness, doesn't wonder.

Amazingly, one person recorded his attempt to settle the matter. He stood on the platform as the man, we'll call him Andre, was losing his head, and as soon as his head flopped into the basket, the curious man reached down and turned it toward him and looked into the eyes. He said he received a look of unquestionable recognition, until the man's eyelids closed. At which point he shouted "Andre!" and the eyes opened and stared directly at him for more than a second before the eyes glazed over in the familiar distant look of a person as they die, and the lids closed again.

The question focuses, at least in the old dispensation, on the matter of where the soul, or the person, the self, resides. Today the closest we might come to agreeing on a substitute for soul (a term perhaps too amorphous or freighted with centuries of parochialism?) is consciousness. Is it solely in the head, the brain, or as we sometimes believe? Is it even possible to speak of one without the other? This must be the reason we are wary of the idea of a soul. It disembodies the central notion of the person as a single, indivisible entity. It suggests that some independent consciousness may borrow this body for a lifetime.

There have been many off-beat experiments in our so-called modern era, in which surgeons have grafted the head of a dog onto the body of another dog and kept it going for some time. You will remember that Walt Disney's and Ted Williams' bodies are both quick frozen in a cryogenic process that anticipates a time when the diseases and aging process that brought them down have been neutralized and they can return to the busy work of hitting home runs and running theme parks. Their heads, I have read, have, for more convenient storage, been separated from their bodies.

What follows is an exploration of a few of the practical issues surrounding this matter.

Anson's Cheatin' Heart

Anson was in his 60s when Our Hero got to know him and like and admire him. Despite his being a clean living American paragon who suffered from heart disease. As a boy Rheumatic Fever had damaged his aortic heart valve and, though they were expecting to be able to replace his valve with a pig valve when it was necessary, his doctor warned him that he shouldn't expect to live beyond 40. This tough Yankee regarded that prognosis as a challenge flung directly in his flinty, Yankee face.

Not only did he graduate from Harvard and Harvard Business School, but he founded his own investment company, moved to suburban New York and commuted daily to Wall Street in a life that the healthiest heart would find taxing. He married and had children. Never smoked or took strong drink, ate only food whose origin he could know for certain. Sex, the other matter normally linked to these cautions, was, for Anson, a practical issue. A matter for, well, for issue. He thought Bill Clinton's excess, lack of impulse-control, was disgusting.

And when Anson was 40, his heart weakened to the point at which he was told that unless he underwent the valve replacement his heart would soon be so seriously compromised that he would become bedridden and die. They believed he had a great chance—90 percent—of surviving the surgery, and perhaps a 70 percent chance of regaining sufficient heart function to return to full strength.

Anson never hesitated. "Do it!" he demanded. They did and he did well. The pig valve worked wonderfully (for Anson, not the pig) and he went on with his busy, successful life. Back to Wall Street, back to weekend hockey in a league of fading prep-school jocks. (But in deference to the valve from a pig that likely never skated, he switched his position on the team from line to goal. He was an awesome goalie.)

113

By the time Anson's path crossed Our Hero's path, Anson had gone through two new pig valves and one of the new mechanical valves made from a space-age material the body seldom rejects. And now his heart was finally showing the fatigue of a muscle that has been artificially propped up for a long time and has lost its own ability to regenerate. Now his doctor (a new, young doctor; his original doctor had long ago died of congestive heart failure) told him he was a candidate for a heart transplant.

"Do it!"

Our Hero, who was his parish priest, visited him at home while Anson was waiting for someone to suffer some sort of catastrophic terminal process (that's medical for get his ass handed to him) that would leave him without the ability to recover, but his heart undamaged.

"So, Anson," Our Hero had a way of cutting to the chase, "what are your chances of getting a heart before yours gives out completely?"

"Great!" You'll have noticed that Anson always, at least when talking about his heart, speaks in sentences that end in an exclamation point. "But I hope it doesn't happen before I get finished building the book cases in our library."

He had an ejection fraction (the measure of the percentage of the blood in the heart ejected with each beat) in single numbers. An athlete's fraction will be in the high 80s or 90s.

When they called him from Massachusetts General Hospital late one wintry night, to tell him they thought they had a heart for him (they always call at least two, sometimes three people waiting for a heart, and do the final close cross matching at the hospital, which means that at least one person will go home a broken-hearted bridesmaid), there was a raging ice storm and his wife drove him across treacherous roads, skidding through intersections, sliding off the road several times in their old Ford station wagon, while Anson, gasping for breath between phrases, sang a song of celebration—("You gotta have heart, you gotta have heart . . . All you really need is heart.")—seemingly with no fear for what he faced.

When they reached the emergency entrance to the hospital, it was 2am and the security guard warily approached the car. He asked if he could be of help. Katherine, Anson's wife, ragged from an hour's near-death drive, shouted (she had thought she was going to speak in a normal voice), "My husband's been called in to receive a heart transplant!"

Though he was annoyed at Katherine's hysteria, unbecoming a Yankee spouse, the sound of the words "heart transplant" sounded so lyrical to Anson that he began singing again. "My heart belongs to Daddy." And laughing. Gasping. Choking.

"Stay right there," the security guard ordered, "while I go get a wheel chair."

"Not on your tintype," Anson protested, "I'm walking in." He opened the car door and stepped out, slipping on the icy driveway, barely regaining his balance, his breath catching. The security guard and Katherine both lurched toward him. Anson held up both hands, palms out, his face resolute. He walked slowly, deliberately, toward the door with the lighted emergency sign above it. The guard followed behind him. Just inside the door Anson lowered himself into a wheelchair, looked up at the guard and said, "Have a heart, my good man, and take me to your bank."

Anson was the perfect match for the heart of a 16-year-old girl who had run her Volkswagen Beatle into a tree on an icy curve in a suburb on Boston's North Shore. When they removed Anson's heart the doctor said it was so flaccid they couldn't have used it for second base on a baseball diamond; it would have just fallen apart the first time someone slid in to break up a double play.

The 16-year-old girl's heart took some time getting used to inhabiting his pure—booze, nicotine, caffeine-free—body. Not to mention his over-60 habit of dwelling in a relatively sex-free zone. For more than a week Anson lay in a semi-coma, babbling incoherently, using language he once washed out his daughter's mouth for using. His upright family feared even more for his reputation than for his survival. Luckily, he was kept in isolation, out of concern his body would reject his heart. His family's fear—that if his body didn't reject the frisky new heart, their friends would reject his frisky new language—was never tested.

When he finally came to himself, the nurse found him propped in his bed, gingerly holding his semi-erect male organ in his curled palm. "Will you look at this?" he invited her. "I can't remember the last time I saw this thing come to life."

The nurse had worked in the transplant unit for several years and was used to behavior that never made its way into the literature for this procedure. "Good for you!" she praised. "I believe you're well on your way to a full recovery."

"And more!" he exclaimed, still hoarse from the tube recently removed from his trachea. "This isn't a recovery; it's a resurrection."

Two weeks later the doctors released Anson and sent him home. He yielded to hospital protocol requiring that he be delivered to the front door in a wheelchair, but as they approached the door he insisted that the volunteer wheeling him stop. He pushed himself out of the wheelchair to a standing position, hesitated for a moment and walked from the corridor, out the door and sat himself in the passenger seat of the old Ford station wagon.

"Who was the last person to get a new heart who walked in and walked out of the hospital?" he asked the nurse from the transplant unit who accompanied him,"

"I do believe you've reset the bar for our entire program," she marveled.

To Katherine's relief (she still worked full time), his interest exceeded his energy, so even though he seemed to have gained the enthusiasm of a blossoming adolescent, he still had the liver, kidneys, lungs and testosterone of a man beyond his feral years.

But the questions seem to double, and triple; does the soul reside in the heart and/or the brain? Is it appropriate to presume Anson's soul was the engine that was in some way driving this epiphenomenon that would cause his final chapter to be quite different from the genteel fade of his peers? And from his previous sixty-some years above ground?

Our Hero visited Anson at home two months after the surgery, and found him in his library tearing out the shelves he had put in before going to the hospital.

"Anson," OH wondered, "what's the scoop here? Wasn't that the project you were so eager to get finished before you went to the hospital?"

"Yep. But a couple of things have happened in the meantime. One is that I thought I was going to die, so I built shelves that would work for Katherine to put her big gardening and decorating books on. In fact I designed this room for her. But now I'm taking it back. And I want shelves that will hold a lot of books, not fewer big ones. The other thing is that I'm looking to have a section on sex in this library. Do you know I had never even seen a copy of Playboy magazine until one of the nurses brought me a copy in the hospital. It's a weird thing; here I am 63 years old and in fact no more sexually active than I was before getting my new heart. Well, maybe a little." His eyes sparkled. In all the years he had known him Our Hero had never seen this side of Anson. "But," Anson went on, "my fantasies are like a great skin flick. (Where did he even learn that expression?) It's as if something of the energy of the girl whose heart I now have, has become a part of my energy. I'm having a blast."

"You thought you were going to die?" Our Hero was incredulous. "But everything you said, the way you handled yourself, made us all think you were the only one who didn't think you might die."

"Right, I know that. That's the way I lived my whole life. Those insane bond issues we underwrote back in the 70s? When everyone told me we were going to lose out shirt? You think I was an iota as confident that they would go as I sounded at the time? When they took off I was the most surprised guy in the firm. Shit, that was my MO; picked it up at Harvard Business School and never looked back. Stood me in pretty good stead I'd say, through a lot of years on Wall Street. Didn't make me a lot of friends, but sure made me a lot of money."

Anson turned toward Our Hero and put down his hammer. The look on Anson's face was new to Our Hero, almost as if Anson was seeing something behind OH, looking through right him to something on the other side of the wall.

"You know something weird, OH? I'm pretty happy I outlived that chapter. Not that I regret it, but I always wondered if maybe there was another dimension I was missing. It wasn't even that I wanted people to like me better, though I did. But it was more that I watched some other people, some sort of like you, OH, and wondered if they were experiencing a whole dimension of life I wasn't."

You get the picture, dear reader. The medical literature on heart transplants mentions personality issues, but they are mostly about depression. One theory is that the brain is blood-oxygen-starved for a period and it takes time for the brain cells to regain their plasticity. Their ability to hold oxygen.

But suppose there is another explanation, or another dimension to the issue—one beyond our understanding of human tissue and personality. Suppose cells, or atoms, or molecules, are as individual and idiosyncratic as we recognize people to be.

The ancient Hebrews believed blood was the seat of life—a pretty sophisticated notion in light of what we now know. Could it be that blood cells, driven and oxygenated by a different set of organs, could carry some new sense, opening possibilities not present when driven by the old apparatus? And of course there are new blood cells, transfused from an unknown third person.

Anson moved to a new city within a year of his transplant and Our Hero, though in touch through email, didn't see him again for some time.

Three years later, when Our Hero visited Anson, he noticed several new things about him. One was his rounded, more feminine face, due in part, no doubt, to the steroids he continued to take to prevent his body from rejecting the new heart. But the softness of his appearance, not only of his previously chiseled features, but the look in his eyes, suggested that something else about him was different, something more subtle. Our Hero asked him about what differences he was aware of.

"Well," Anson began thoughtfully, which itself was a marked change from his old Wall St. days when his responses came rapidly and with a kind of military certainty, "I like people better than I used to. I always used to feel impatient when people began telling me stories about themselves, as if they were taking time away from my being productive. Now I love to settle down and listen. At first I thought it was because I have less energy, but that's not it. It's a lot more than that."

"How about the sex thing, Anson?" Our Hero dared to ask because Anson had brought it up in a recent email.

Anson smiled a far-off reflective smile and said, "Funny you should ask; I was just thinking about that before you arrived. Katherine probably wouldn't like it much, but I find I have sexual feelings for lots of people, and not just for women either. At first I was sort of freaked out about that. I mean I went to boarding school when the worst thing you could be called was "queer." You know, now, I think I would call myself queer, not necessarily about sex, but about all sorts of things. And it makes me wonder about all the people I dumped on all those years. I'll be straight-on with you." he looked Our Hero in the eye. "OH, I wouldn't have given you the time of day before now. Fact is I didn't. I was tolerant because you had a position of respect and authority, but I thought you were a dip. You know those vestry meetings—when I was on the church vestry and you were rector? Well, the reason I was always late was because I couldn't stand all that touchy-feely shit you put us through at the beginning of the meeting. Before we got to the real business."

Our Hero laughed. "You were pretty transparent about that, Anson."

"Yeah, well, I really didn't care. But the way I feel now, I could let those balance sheets hang. I used to bury my head in them, to wall myself off when the meeting got into all that touchy feely stuff,. You must admit, we had some hellish long meetings and we never really resolved the financial problems."

"Nice to see your old Anson is still in there."

Now Anson laughed. "Man those old habits are hard to break."

"You want to talk about what feels different to you now, Anson? Not only the sexual stuff, but your body, your heart; can you actually feel a difference you can talk about?"

Anson looked uncertain, then smiled. "The really weird thing is that I was totally unaware of my body before. I mean I knew if I was hurt or tired, but that was about it. I couldn't have told you what I was feeling—what emotion was going through me. I only knew if I felt like I was gaining or losing. That was it."

Our Hero watched Anson shift in his chair. His eyes misted, Our Hero had never seen that in him before. "You know, OH, oh God; this is still hard stuff for me to talk about, but I want to . . . I feel like I've been born again. No, not the hysterical religious way, but almost literally, like I've been given a whole new life.

"Feelings, in my body? I've got a million of them. I feel a tingling in my head, behind both ears, like there was fresh blood running through there. Sometimes I think I can even hear it. If you can imagine what the opposite of a headache would feel like, maybe like a sore muscle getting back its elasticity, it would be sort of like that. My eyes seem sharper, younger. I can read the phone book without magnifiers, which I haven't done for 20 years. My scalp, my bald pate, feels warm even when I go outside on a cold day. I look at myself in the mirror, which my old Yankee self thought was conceited. Now I do it a lot, and I see the same-appearing guy I remember. But now he looks back at me completely differently. It's like being reintroduced to myself."

"Holy shit, Anson, have you told anyone else about all this? I mean this could do even more for the heart transplant business than curing the rejection problem."

"Well, no. First of all you're the first person to ask. And maybe I wasn't ready yet, or the right person to talk to hadn't come around before. But it isn't all wonderful. I mean I am thrilled about it, and amazed. But it's no small thing to find yourself a whole new person just when you're getting ready to pack it in."

"What's the hardest part?"

"All the stuff I feel so powerfully that I used to think was bad."

"Like?"

"Like feeling like fucking every person I feel close to. Didn't Jimmy Carter confess that as one of his besetting sins?"

"Yeah, he did. And what did you think about that at the time?"

"I thought he was an asshole, both to let himself have all those feelings, and then to talk about them. I still think he's an asshole. I still think he blew both the Iran-hostage thing and let interest-rates get out of control. You see I still have some rational Republican judgment in me, but not because of those old feelings. I mean, Jesus, I have these new feelings, all stirred up—sexual, alive—a hundred times a day." Anson shifted to one side, looked away.

"You having one now?"

"Oh give me a break, OH. And don't flatter yourself."

They both laughed.

THE OLD RANDY WRITER

One sunny summer day in Vermont, in the summer of 2000, a summer that saw precious few sunny days, OH walked down the hill from his 19th Century farmhouse on the pond to the construction site where the crumbling WPA bridge was finally being replaced. OH had initially been unhappy about plans to build a new bridge. Even though the old one was held together by rebar that had been wrapped precariously around the crumbling concrete edges. Most townspeople, and the various Vermont state agencies, agreed a good ice dam could take out the bridge. OH liked the old bridge. Like most flatlanders,—people who had moved to Vermont from what they regarded as more civilized and less desirable places—he wanted things left as they were. The school bus drivers who crossed the bridge several times a day with a bus full of local children took a less sentimental view. As did the state of Vermont.

The project was on the books four years before work was begun. OH received engineering drawings, site visits from archaeologists, environmentalists and several sentimental fellow-flatlanders opposed to change in their adopted home. OH loved looking down onto the bridge from his screen porch. At the opposite end of the 20-acre pond he watched the beavers swim from their lodge toward his house. On the bank beneath his porch they foraged for green shoots and for more substantial material for shoring up their dwelling.

OH had wondered if he could really live in a remote rural town of 500 people. He loved going weekends from Boston, but he knew that was not the same as living there full time. Long before Chevy Chase filmed his movie spoof of the woman who made a disastrous move to Vermont, thinking she was ready to simplify her life (OH didn't find it very funny), he fretted about whether he was up to it.

He couldn't really think of what it was he would be missing. Despite his intellectual pretensions, he rarely went to museums or the theater, openly hated opera, and rarely ventured into Boston traffic for a Red Sox game. Still, something nagged him, made him wonder if he was being as unrealistic and sentimental as the woman in the Chevy Chase movie.

His anxiety was triggered when a friend, hearing of his plans to move to the tiny, rural Vermont town, asked him if he would be the only resident there with a mouthful of his own teeth.

Child that he was of the 60s, he had no idea what he really believed or wanted or valued. Except affirmation. He understood his parents had thought affirmation was the fabric from which ruined lives were woven. He supposed they had loved him, perhaps as irrationally as he loved his Norfolk Terrier. But it had been a matter of strict discipline with them that they never display that love in a way that might cause OH to think it was due him. That he should expect to receive it in the normal course of life without doing something to earn it. Like Pavlov's dog, OH was to receive positive conditioning, approval, open love, only after having achieved something to earn it. Thus he would be toughened for the way the world really works—reward for achievement, punishment for failure.

After endless hours of psychotherapy, OH had come to understand, even appreciate his parents' intentions, and in his best moments he could see that their method of parenting had in fact made him tough and able to achieve in the rough-and-tumble world of free enterprise.

But when it came to his own desires, he was clueless. He was a master at discerning what others wanted from him, and mostly (he thought) happy to provide it. Which made him a successful parish minister, but it left him in a vacuum when it came to choosing for himself. Or discerning his vocation. Hearing the call of his own hungry heart.

So the move to Vermont was a step into the abyss. It was built on stories he had heard of high powered men tiring of the rat race and making a radical move to a venue that provided sustenance for their souls. Releasing their death grip on their career paths. It sounded heroic to him. He had always wished he might make some heroic move before the flab of old age made such a move inevitable rather than brave.

And one day OH was reading a profile of Saul Bellow, an author he admired. He loved Bellow's writing, most of which OH had read and a portion of which he could follow. Bellow, a tough Jew from Chicago who had been married multiple times, was portrayed in the profile as a man who cared only about his own work. Anyone who wanted to be in his life would have to be subordinate to his writing. They would have to actually provide some sort of support for that effort. In other words, Bellow used people for his own ends, and made no bones about it. Nor apologies.

Oh was in awe of anyone that clear and focused. And free of worry about what others wanted from him.

What's more Saul Bellow had won the Nobel prize.

The profile was in the New Yorker. The New Yorker had once published a Letter-To-The Editor OH had written. It was an ego boost. As he read the piece about Bellow OH sensed the seemingly unbridgeable gap between the relentless focused toughness of the old Nobel laureate and his own pathetic expenditure of his life-energy seeking to please people and gain approval.

The writer of the article was afraid to tape his interviews with Bellow, or even take notes. Bellow had been so difficult and disagreeable about giving him the interview that he was certain if he seemed to be preserving the conversation in any way, Bellow would just stop talking.

So the interviewer was trying all sorts of mental tricks to help himself remember what Bellow said. And when he finally left Bellow's house, as soon as he was out of sight, he pulled over to the side of the road and stopped to write down everything before his memory failed. He described the place he stopped next to a large pond on a winding rural road in a remote part of southern Vermont. "There was," he wrote, "a sign nailed to a tree by the pond. It said 'Quiet. Beavers at work. Lil' Becky Beaver, Mayor'."

"Holy Shit!" OH shouted, slapping the magazine across his knee, "Saul Bellow lives above the pond by our house!"

And that had cemented the deal. That and OH having been told that every landowner in town got a free plot in the town cemetery.

On the day in question, now three years and a thousand traumas after having moved to the tiny village, OH was talking to the construction workers building the new bridge, that summer's diversion from his work on his novel. Their conversation was about the capricious weather gods who had chosen the summer they built the new bridge to visit the heaviest rainfall on record. The temporary dam they had built upstream had washed out twice, adding at least a month onto the projected date of completion, which suited OH. His conversations with the workers more than made up for there being no TV reception at his house. He wished the job would drag on through the winter.

This day cars, unable to travel across either the old or the new bridge, people had to park and walk across. As OH and the workers watched, a black Lincoln Town Car pulled up in front of his house uphill from the construction site. From the car emerged a young man, a woman in her 30s with a 2-year-old child, and an old man in his 80s.

"Know who that is?" OH asked the workers.

"No, who is it?"

"That's Saul Bellow."

"Oh yeah? Who's Saul Bellow?"

"Probably the most famous living American fiction writer. He won the Nobel Prize."

"Oh yeah? What's the Nobel Prize?"

"The most important prize you can receive for writing."

"Huh. Who're those people with him?"

"Well, the young man is his literary assistant, goes with him everywhere, drives his car, edits his writing, puts his writing on the computer. And the woman is his wife. I think she's his fifth wife. Pretty, isn't she?"

"Uh huh. How old is he?"

"83."

"And his wife?"

"I think she's around 35."

"Who's baby is that?"

"That's their baby."

"You mean the old writer and the young wife? That's their baby?"

"Uh huh."

They all stood watching as the trio passed them, walking slowly, the baby—a new walker—grasping her mother's finger to stay upright, and Bellow—a veteran but unsteady walker—had his arm hooked through hers. OH had only seen the great man a couple of times, and he reveled in being this close, thrilled at sharing their rural setting, two writers. The construction foreman removed his hard hat and scratched his forehead, waiting until Saul Bellow and his family were out of earshot, before speaking.

"They didn't give him that prize for writing."

THE ATOMIC/CELLULAR THEORY

"Suppose you were to have the long imagined look into what happens when you die?"

The question reminded OH of the story he had heard about Errol Flynn's dying. He was in his 80s. He lived with his girlfriend who was in her 20s. The two of them were lying by their pool in southern California, tanning. She heard him groan. She looked over, his body seemed to have relaxed, gone limp. His chest moved a little. She leaned over him and and called his name. He spoke his last words in this life; "Hell, dying's not so much."

The most interesting thing about the question is that the one who asked it of OH was what is known in religious circles as a Primate. A funny title, because in ordinary language it refers to a creature thought to occupy a rung beneath the rung our kind occupies on the evolutionary scale. But in religious talk it refers to one who sits on the highest hierarchical rung.

This Primate—dressed in civvies, not his golden threads—and OH were on a small deserted beach in the south Pacific. It was an interlude in one of those high powered conferences people of high station attend in exotic places so they can think and speak without the distracting rigors of their ordinary duties. OH was there not as a peer to the exalted conferees, but as a consultant observer, which made him less threatening to the Primate who was asking a question millions of the world's faithful assumed he had answered long since. OH felt compassion for Primate, having to wait all these years for a moment when he could talk about such a thing. So in his response he decided to try a gentle tack.

"Odd you should ask," he paused, looking out over the blue/green sea, hoping to add weight to what he was about to say. "Last week, after the fires that burned half of Southern California, when the ash blew in from the east, covering every surface in San Diego, my doctor said to me, 'You realize, these ashes have DNA in them."

"Really?" Primate responded, his sagging aging belly hiding the waist band of his boxer bathing trunks, "meaning exactly what?"

OH considered Primate's furry silver gray chest hair. "Well, have you ever wondered whether that beach chair you are sitting on might have a cell in the wood that once was part of the manger in which Jesus was placed after his birth?"

Primate squinted as he looked into the tropical sun hovering over the horizon. "A little far-fetched, don't you think?"

"Odds against maybe, but far-fetched? I wouldn't say so. What do you suppose becomes of your cells after they slough off, or after you die?"

"I don't suppose I have the faintest notion."

"Well, give it a try. Might move you a little closer to the answer to your question."

"What about faith? What about Jesus' resurrection? Lazarus?" Primate's question sounded petulant, impatient with OH's toying with him.

"Can you answer a question with a question? Even if I thought your question could be answered, it wouldn't have any bearing on mine. Jesus lived to be 33, so he must have sloughed off something like four bodies worth of cells. What happened to them?"

"They fell on the ground, I suppose."

"And just stayed there? Do you think those atoms are still blowing around in the dust in the Middle East? You've been there; ever had the sense you were walking around on Jesus or Lazarus?"

"How would you gain such a sense?"

"How do you know you're hungry? Or horny?"

"Your body tells you, provides physical sensations."

"Do the atoms on your feet have senses?"

"So you think the continuity we all wonder so much about has to do with what happens to the materials that make up our bodies?"

"Would that seem like a disappointment to you?"

"Well, I would say it's considerably less than we have been advertising to the faithful these past couple of millennia."

"I'm not so sure. Let me suggest that we're getting into much richer territory than the church has classically probed. Do you think people actually buy that stuff about heaven and dead people being pretty much the same as they have been in life?"

"I'm afraid they may. I did until I went to seminary."

"No offense, Primate, but you're an old man. Ninety percent of the world's people are younger than you are and they have lived through a history that came too late to form you. But not them. For many if not most, of them, it's as if they had gone through the seminary training you had by the time they reached puberty. So perhaps their concern is not focused so much on whether their ego can survive forever. They've already stuffed their ego until it is so bloated it feels like a burden. They're looking for some way to become disentangled from what it is we old folks are trying so hard to hang onto."

The sun had dropped so it was now only a few degrees above the horizon and Primate shivered, a combination of the falling temperature and an injection of cold reality his usual routine spared him.

"What an odd thought. A world filled with post-seminary theological cynics."

"Not cynics, Primate, realists. Ever wonder why the Dalai Lama draws those crowds of young people wherever he goes? Maybe you heard him say that if some scientist showed him he was wrong about something he believes, he would change his beliefs? That's a long way from putting Galileo in chains because his investigation cast doubt on the view of the universe the church imposed on its followers."

"I was quite struck by The Dalai Lama's saying that. I have spent time with him. He seems quite at home with himself, doesn't he?"

"You know what is the most hopeful sign that you may actually find some response to the question you asked me?"

"No; I'd pretty much given up hoping for that."

"Well, of course it won't be an answer in the classical sense you may have been hoping for. But the hopeful sign is that you asked the question. You know the last time a Primate asked such a question of me?"

Now Primate looked really interested. He never dared raise these sorts of things with his fellow world leaders, both because he thought he was already supposed to have resolved them, and because he worried they might be further along in their spiritual maturity than he was. "No," he responded, "I don't. But I'd be very interested to know and to know who it was and when."

"Never," OH laughed. "You're the first Primate to ask me. Now what that tells me is that you're the most likely Primate to reach some sort of resolution to your question. If that's any comfort. It likely won't advance you in your world, but it may make your sleeping easier. And your dying."

"And, God help me," Primate's voice was urgent, "it may make sleeping a lot scarier. Not that I have been counting on ascending bodily into heaven. But I guess I have been thinking there must be something to what we have been sponsoring as the hope for eternal life for a couple of millennia."

"Sarcasm is good, Primate. It shows that you are engaged at a very primal level." OH laughed. "But then I guess you would be engaged at a primal level, huh?"

Primate looked annoyed, then smiled, then laughed aloud. "Jesus Christ, this is so silly, this worrying about what I am supposed to be thinking. So, tell me, what do you really think? About life and death?"

"I think it's a near miraculous cycle we've wandered into," OH offered. "Something that has always interested me is whether we have made any choice in being a part of this, or is it an unlikely chance confluence of factors. The problem with most religious schemes is that they are too small, not nearly grand enough. They are ego driven which means they use our species, or even our psyches as the measure of the whole scheme."

"Since we're doing the measuring, how could we do otherwise?"

"It's called empathy, Primate, the ability to stand outside one's self and see things from a different perspective."

"I've heard of it." Primate let himself laugh at himself. "I'm just not sure I have it in me."

"If you didn't, you'd believe in your own bullshit and we wouldn't be having this conversation. It always amazes me how much you spooks can conceal about yourselves in order to get ahead. Then the question becomes, get ahead of whom?"

"You mean what, not whom," Primate protested,

"I don't think so. The first step is to look around when you're still very young, and identify your competition. I'm sure you did that."

"I did in fact. Still do sometimes, even though I'm at the end and have no higher rung on the ladder to climb. Weird that I can still so this, but it's a lifelong habit by now."

OH felt he could press on. "So, Primate, what is it you're hoping it's going to be like when you die? By the way, when do you intend to die?"

"I'm nearing 80 and I have always thought I'd make it to 85. I wish I could tell you what I hope. I guess I hope the way I've spent my life will look like it was a good way, that it counted for something."

"Like what?"

"Like for good, like I left it better than I found it. The world."

"How would you know?"

"There are more people who are happy, fewer who are suffering?"

"The way your voice rose at the end there makes me think that was a question."

"Look, OH, are you a total cynic? Do you not think anything really matters?"

"Primate, you are the one who asked the question. If you don't want to hear what I think, or if you already have locked yourself into another opinion, we could talk about the weather. Or whether it is a good idea to ordain gay people?"

"Now you're fucking with my head."

"Listen, Primate, I have respect for you and for your high office, and compassion for what you must endure to occupy that office. What I think is that we humans are way too hooked on our own parochial perspective, thinking that because we have come up with the notion of consciousness and language, we know more than other creatures, even pretend to know what is going on in this creation."

"Do you know,"—OH was on a roll—"they did experiments recently with some dolphin trying to determine their level of intelligence? They worked out a seemingly simple trial in which they asked the dolphins to jump out of the water and make a sound. When they did it the way the experimenters wanted, they would receive a fish. In the beginning the dolphins did great—or what the human experimenters interpreted as great. But then they began making different, original sorts of sounds, more subtle than they had been taught by their human handlers. Finally the dolphin were jumping out of the water without seeming to make any sound at all. And the experimenters assumed that, without more significant reinforcement of the desired behavior, the dolphins were unable to replicate it."

"Well, when they reviewed tapes of the training they put sophisticated sound detecting equipment on the tapes and discovered that not only were the original different sounds of varying frequencies and decibels, but when they thought the dolphins had stopped making sounds, they in fact were emitting sound at a frequency inaudible to the range of human hearing."

"It seems that while the humans were testing the intelligence of the dolphins, the dolphins were testing the hearing range of the humans."

"And your point?" Primate's expression tightened. "I don't see what this has to do with the question I asked about what happens when we die."

OH smiled carefully hoping to reassure Primate to think he wasn't laughing at him. He sighed. "Primate, you are a very smart man, and, even more important to me, a good man, honestly concerned about reality despite all the trappings surrounding you that are meant to cushion you from too stark an encounter with reality.

"What the dolphin experiment says to me is that all our conclusions about how things are, are tentative and conditioned by our own fears and wishes. And projections. And that we tend to doubt or simply ignore any reality that is beyond our reckoning.

"You understand, OH," Primate's voice lowered, signaling his intensity, "what we're really talking about here? I have an irregular heart beat, a semi-dormant prostate cancer, high blood pressure, an aortic aneurysm, a balloon that could burst anytime. This is no longer academic to me. I expect to be dead soon."

"You're going to love dying, Primate. Better than sex."

"And how do you know?"

"If we were living in Old testament times I would say God told me. Today I have no vocabulary for it. So you'll just have to decide whether you think I really know something or I'm blowing smoke. I know. And all this stuff we have been talking about, such a big deal to us now, and quite properly, will become insignificant. Well, maybe not insignificant. Interesting, but no need for us to manage and fret over it."

Primate began to weep, silently at first, tears falling down his cheeks, then his shoulders heaving, giving way to loud sobbing. OH watched from a foot away, made no move to embrace or console him. The crying lasted a minute or two. Snot ran from Primate's nose as he struggled to regain his breath. The tropical sun dropped beneath the horizon behind him. OH thought there might be a green flash as the sun disappeared from the cloudless sky. Primate took several deep intakes of breath, sighed and finally looked up at OH.

OH smiled at him.

"How was that?" he asked.

"Sublime," Primate said, "the most powerful energy that has run through my body in many years. You know, it has been longer since I last cried than since my last orgasm."

"Same energy when it works right," OH said.

"So right," Primate agreed. "I am so grateful for this time with you, OH. What could I ever do to thank you?"

"Die happily."

Primate stepped into OH's arms and they embraced. Primate, several inches shorter than OH, raised his face to OH and they kissed a long, lips-to-lips kiss. OH felt a faint pressure where Primate's aging member stirred against him. Primate pulled his head back and looked up at OH, taking his face into both hands, looking deeply into his eyes. Then he dropped his hands and took a step back.

"Go in peace," OH said.

"Thanks be to God," Primate responded.

OH Goes to Ground Zero

When the second plane collided with the second tower of the World Trade Center, OH walked outside and gazed into the sky, an impulse he didn't quite understand but couldn't resist. He had only ever seen the towers from the distance as he drove across the Throgs Neck Bridge far down the East River,. Perhaps some piece of his internal radar sensed that the second plane had been commandeered by terrorists almost directly over his 19th century farmhouse, at 22,000 feet and climbing. His consciousness was far too noisy at that moment for him to register anything beneath.

Most of the week before, OH had tried several different ways to eradicate a nest of white wasps beneath the hydrangea bush in his front yard. The three men painting his house called the nest to his attention just before he would have run the lawn mower over it. OH bought three bombs to spray into the hole at dusk. He bombed the nest three evenings in a row. The third time he placed a large rock on top of the hole, thinking perhaps a few strays hadn't made it back to the nest before he sprayed. Each morning the nest would be a center of activity. The third morning a newly excavated hole provided access and egress for what looked to be more wasps than ever.

OH turned to Bummy, his long-time caretaker who had bailed him out of more flatlander dilemmas than he cared to admit in the 20 years he had owned the rural farmhouse.

"Well, if the bomb didn't work," Bummy suggested (nothing defeated Bummy, the original can-do guy), "put some gasoline in there tonight and light it. Then, when the flames die out, pour oil into the hole. That'll do it."

So he did. Made a pretty sight just as darkness fell. The next morning the hole was scorched, the grass black and dead for five yards in every direction. Which made the white wasps easier to see as they buzzed busily in and out of the hole.

OH turned next to Tracey, the dairy farmer whose tenure in the cow-barn had tuned his inner sense to a reality and rhythm of non-human beings in startling ways OH had not experienced in any other human.

"You really want to be rid of them?" Tracey asked, broad smile filling his handsome face.

"Uh huh."

"Well then, move your house. They were there before your house. Maybe not in that exact spot. Chances are they'll move off when it no longer suits them. Could even be in your lifetime. Who knows?"

OH had nearly forgotten that same advice Tracey had given him about the skunk that nested beneath his front stoop the year the pond flooded the neighbor's septic system.

"Probably got too wet where she was. It'll dry out in time; then she'll likely move again. Hardly ever stays in one place more than a couple of years."

All this flooded back into OH's overstuffed consciousness as he looked high up to where the American Airlines plane, carrying people who boarded at the same gate where he usually boarded at Logan Airport to fly to California, had changed course, perplexing the two air traffic controllers, one of whom was just releasing and the other embracing the plane on their radar screens.

White wasps, skunks, Saudi martyrs, all mortally bonded to OH at that moment. He decided he would walk down the hill half way into town and get Jane, who had a barber chair in her kitchen, to cut his hair. The connections were burning their way into his awareness with an intensity he felt he might be unable to endure. He tried to focus on his breath, his steps, as he breathed and walked slowly, deliberately, across the bridge the state had just rebuilt, losing the temporary dam downstream twice in the heaviest rainfall in memory. He turned left and passed Ranslow's house on the far side of the road, marking the moment several years before, when their building supply store had delivered the materials that they assured him would soon resurrect his house that had been neglected for the past decade.

So he and Jane watched the twin towers scatter their detritus across the tip of Manhattan Island. Jane was standing behind OH trimming the curls on the back of his neck. Luckily she stopped clipping as she leaned across him, forcing his head down. The two of them remained in silence; the reporter gasped audibly, unprofessionally. Finally Jane provided a Vermont perspective:

"I really don't think there are enough of us up here for them to come bother with."

[At that moment neither of them was consciously aware that the second plane had turned course—under the control of amateur pilots from Saudi Arabia—almost directly over their heads. North Adams, Massachusetts— the site from which Jacksonville, Vermont gets weather forecasts—shelters a tiny dirt runway alongside Mt. Greylock, Massachusetts' tallest peak. Twenty-two-thousand feet directly above that runway American Airlines flight #84 made her sharp left turn and took the relentless lethal aim that would define President Bush's understanding of why God had chosen him to be President. God—the erstwhile Texan would decide—had chosen him despite the American voters having chosen the wooden-faced vice president. It confirmed Bush's born-again belief that God's will trumps even the will of the voters. At that moment President Bush made a sacred covenant with God to fulfill his destiny and eradicate the evil that made war on the symbols of America's financial and military supremacy. President Bush's medieval sense of his vocation would alter the terms of the entire planet's course for the next many years.]

"No shit?" OH's exhale sounded more like a question. As it escaped his lips he realized he had never used profanity in front of Jane, nor had he ever heard her use any. If Jane was shocked by his language, he couldn't detect it. "Maybe that's why we're all here," he offered.

"Not me," Jane countered, not taking her eyes from the TV, "I'm here because my Dad was a dairy farmer and I was born here. How come you're here?"

OH and Jane just never had conversations beyond weather and how the kids were doing in college. But then they'd never known the country's two tallest buildings to be knocked down by people whose visitor's visas had expired.

"Likely, come to think of it, that's the reason as much as any." OH lifted his hand from beneath the striped table cloth that protected him from falling hair and pointed, with a shaking forefinger at the image on the TV. "All my life I've been scared of violence. Vermont always seemed so peaceful—more cows than people, and all."

"You're pretty sheltered, you flatlanders, from a lot of the stuff we natives live through." OH was beginning to grow uneasy at the conversation, what with Jane wielding a pair of scissors as the horror at what they had been watching on the tiny TV began to give way to anger. "You know those drug dealers who live in the house at the bottom of the hill?" OH had heard rumors but he figured there was no way their town of under 500 could support drug dealers. He remained silent, waiting for Jane to show her hand. "They threatened the people across the street two nights ago; threatened to burn their house down if they called the cops one more time. You know who burned down the academy building on top of the hill on the other side of town? Peaceful, huh?"

Two weeks later, at a conference on Science and Religion in Cambridge, in Memorial Church in Harvard Yard, OH learned that the images he was seeing on the 12-inch black and white TV were being taken by a church cinematographer who had been bored stiff filming a conversation a block from Ground Zero with Rowan Williams, an erudite English cleric who would soon find himself appointed Archbishop of Canterbury. When the first plane hit the tower, the camera-man abandoned his project, called in to the local ABC affiliate and said he was going outside to film what he could. The station just happened to have a truck nearby and provided a feed directly to the network.

Three years later, when the delegates to the convention of the Episcopal Diocese of New Hampshire elected as their bishop a gay man in a partnered relationship, Archbishop Williams was overheard by his chaplain to say,

"Take me back to Ground Zero."

When there are terrorists around relativism gets a bad name.

RED TAG SPECIAL

OH fell into conversation of an afternoon on a main street in downtown La Jolla, California, with a wo/man who had intrigued him for years. Some years earlier in a long exchange with a transgendered woman in South Carolina he had learned not to trust his impression of which gender the person seemed, at first glance. The South Carolina woman was born a hermaphrodite in England where the law insisted that such a person be raised male He had undergone surgery at the Johns Hopkins Gender Clinic to become an anatomical woman. She had even later conceived and borne a child.

[*N.B. A book has recently been published about the South Carolina woman that suggests she may have been a fraud. Does it ever strike you as odd that a) people would choose identities that cause them nothing but scorn and ostracism, and b) that other people would have such a large stake in challenging their identity that they would devote the energy required to research and write a book about them? I remain in awe of the South Carolina woman, no matter how she came to be whom and what she was, and of the wo/man you are meeting in this piece.*]

So when OH first saw Sara on the street corner, on a rainy winter morning, the only conclusions he permitted himself was that, based on the way he/she shifted from foot to foot, she was likely schizophrenic. And poor. Sara was tall, over six feet, and solidly built, well over 200 pounds. Because her head was shrouded in a hood to protect her from the rain (though he remembered that she almost always wore the hood up even in warm sunny weather), OH could not tell whether she had long or short hair. He could see that Sara had several days growth of a dark beard.

She wore a loose fitting cotton dress that swirled around her ankles as her weight fell first on one foot and then the other. The material was of a repeated floral pattern, cream background, yellow flowers, maybe roses.

Sara wore work boots, laces untied, white athletic socks pulled up a couple of inches above the boots, contrasting with the dark curly hair on her legs.

She never begged for money, though OH and others sometimes gave her a dollar or more. She never looked directly at him when he handed her the money, but she smiled slightly and said "Thank you" so nearly inaudibly that OH wasn't sure he had heard her right the first few times.

That rainy morning Sara was standing on a corner, head held low as if to let the rain drain off the visor of her hood instead of directly into her eyes. OH wondered why she didn't take just a few steps to the porch sheltering the ATM machine on the same corner. But she didn't. On other cold or rainy mornings she always stayed in the open, exposed. OH was always struck by how calm and within herself Sara seemed, even when water dripped off the brim of her hood onto her nose soaking into her beard.

Propped next to Sara was a metal shopping basket on wheels, the kind old people who no longer drive and don't have kids or neighbors to take them shopping, use to carry their groceries back to their apartments. The basket contained an eclectic collection; an old computer hard drive, an umbrella she never opened, a box that once held Pampers, a six pack of empty Guinness Extra Stout bottles, several opaque plastic bags of the sort that get caught in tree limbs and flap dispiritedly in the breeze, a copy of Mary Baker Eddy's **Science and Health With Key to the Scriptures**, a Groucho Marx face mask with the nose, glasses and eyebrows, and blankets that were, as always, wet and dirty.

OH passed Sara every day on his walk to his writing station. He could mark the exact day and moment when he realized that he had fallen in love with him, um, her. Whatever. Truly, it didn't matter.

It was a cloudless March morning, temperature in the low 60s. OH had an extra spring in his step, probably because the marine layer that had shrouded the coastal town for almost a week had lifted and the breeze blew out of the east, causing the surf to kick up a spray that caused occasional rainbows and lifted his spirits. When he saw Sara that morning, she appeared to have cleaned herself up, new socks maybe. He reached into his pocket and pulled out a $20 bill and approached her carefully, respectfully. She didn't acknowledge him. When he drew close enough to hand her the bill, he reached out, but she continued to look down at her feet. He stood awkwardly, realizing he, too, was shifting his weight from one foot to the other, and wondered if anyone was watching. What if they thought he was assaulting her?

He tucked the $20 in the pocket of her jersey, and, without knowing he was going to, took a step closer, embraced her and kissed her on her rough cheek. OH was nearly knocked over by her musty, moldy odor.

"Good for you," Sara said, so softly that, had OH's embrace not positioned his ear almost directly over her mouth, he could not have made out what she said. He stepped back.

"Thank you," OH responded.

Sara continued to look down.

Had she been Madonna, naked, OH would not have been more aroused. He left her and walked south on Girard Street, aware of every leaf on every tree. As he passed the huge glass windows of Classic Cars he stopped to look at the Maserati coupe convertible he had always admired. It had been in the window for several weeks, a glossy green, deeper than the British racing green of a Porsche, with leather seats nearly the color of the animal that had given his life for them.

Hanging from the rear view mirror an oversized red tag advertised, SPECIAL SALE! $79,995!

Looking back at where he had come from, OH could just barely see Sara four blocks down the street. She hadn't moved. He knew she was shifting her weight though he couldn't make it out from this distance. He pictured taking Sara for a wind-in-the-hair ride up the curving road climbing Mt. Soledad, the two of them leaning into every turn in his cut-rate Maserati.

THE LAST TEMPTATION OF OH
THE F WORD

Hard to remember how it had happened. And almost un-happened. OH grew up in a conventionally religious family. He guessed. They went to church. His father had gone to a religious boarding school where the headmaster, a monk, was his lifelong mentor. And tormentor. But his father had never been drawn to poverty, or chastity. So he became a businessman. For which he felt guilty. A Philistine. As penance OH's father became an active layman in whatever Episcopal Church was nearby. And he was, always, best friends with the Rector.

OH found his part in all this full of weird contradictions. He became an acolyte when he was 9 and carried candles and the cross in procession, and sometimes, when he got a little older, even helped the clergy with the holy mysteries, the Mass. All that stirred him up in ways he couldn't express.

He figured he was an instinctive hysteric. In the sense Freud used the term. Loved that rush, though he never could figure out its source. The ceremony, the uniforms, the promise of something big and unnamed behind all the regalia.

But the things everyone else seems to think church was about bored him. The readings didn't seem to matter much. The liturgy, unless it was packed with ceremony, struck him as something everyone in church put up with. The expressions on the faces of the faithful suggested tedium. The music was heavy. Though he liked it when the organ, blowing air through those huge bass pipes, set up sympathetic vibrations with his heart.

He wondered what to make of the clergy who spoke in weighty Gothic voice, as if their normal voices were inadequate to carry the gravity of what they were saying. Yet when the clergy came to OH's house to visit his parents, and drank the dark-brown bourbons that his parents fancied, they became a lot of fun. And not Gothic. And they challenged the Eisenhower Republicanism that OH heard his father mouth without much conviction. Which made his mother throw her head back and laugh as she seldom did otherwise. OH loved it when she did that, as if she was alive in there after all.

OH was sent to his father's religious boarding school. Only he flunked out after a couple of miserable years and went to another, gentler, kinder, less rigorously religious school. From that time, age 16, the year Eisenhower defeated Adlai Stevenson for the second time, until four years later, when Jack Kennedy miraculously and wondrously beat Nixon with the help of old Joe Kennedy's relatively cheap purchase of a few votes in Chicago, it just never occurred to OH that he had any interest in religion. Politics, civil rights, sex, yes. But religion, no.

Or was it that he felt angry, betrayed by the promises religion made and failed to deliver?

Like providing an answer to the question—How come we're here? Or, What's that hunger for merging with a woman, sometimes seemingly any woman, got to do with being good? Or God? Or with feeling dangerously, passionately alive? And, How do you decide what is good anyway? And, How about failure? Is God prepared to cushion OH from the most terrible prospect of all, the likelihood of his failing at life?

Then, weeks past his 18th birthday, in the same week, he read **The Last Temptation of Christ**, by the Greek, Nikos Kazantzakis, and **The Idea of the Holy**, by the German, Rudolf Otto. Between them the two books reorganized OH's picture of the world and what he was to do with the mystery of life having landed in his lusty lap.

The Last Temptation, though focused on Jesus' longing for Mary Magdalene as a temptation Jesus resisted, gave OH permission to join body and sex with hunger for God. Or maybe understand they were so entangled that they could never be separated. Over the next 60 years or so, OH would understand his sexual hunger as a gift he was to offer to a woman and to himself, a gift from God to God. And only once, in a disaster that nearly destroyed him, did he find a woman who understood it as he did. Not long after that brief encounter, the woman left her husband and entered into a relationship with another woman. OH could see that he and the woman had undergone a gender reversal, in which his feminine and her masculine became magnets for each other. He never again attempted to solve the riddle of male vs. female sexuality. And he never doubted that the whole matter was best described in the Genesis story's terse description of the creation of our species: "So God created humankind in God's own image, male and female God created the human."

[You will have noticed, gentle reader, that I have chosen gender language about God that may seem at first silly and trendy, avoiding, wherever possible, using the male or female gender for God. I regard it as essential to the puzzle we are all wanting to solve, the nature of God and the way in which we are in God's image. In the modern western world it makes perfect sense to refer to God as He/Him because the male has, historically, dominated. But as the modern western world morphs into post-modern, not only its experience of reality, but of the balance of male and female, the need to use gender neutral language becomes not just politically correct and desirable, but necessary.]

And it turns one of the most provocative suggestions into a profound promise of divine creative possibility; Why don't you go fuck yourself?

Behold, the image of God is male and female, and generation is bound up within God. God, reality, is the only source of life. All else is illusion. Impotent. Perhaps the sex drive is in fact the urge to merge, to live out the fullness of which each of us is partial. There are only a couple of species that, truly androgynous, have this ability to reproduce within themselves, requiring no outside offering. The last temptation of Jesus, in Kazantzakis' story, and in ours, is the temptation to try to sate the hunger for becoming God. It is the prohibition in the first of the 10 Commandments.

And it is what you are being dared to try when someone suggests you try to fuck yourself. Only God can do that. Our attempts, trivialized in such works as **Women Are From Venus, Men Are From Mars**, always end in grief. But the issue never recedes. Because we come so close. Hermaphrodites, gay couples, rouse the hope and fear in all of us that such a thing might actually be possible.

Make no mistake; this matter has to do with the most primitive and inextinguishable hunger in us. We think our ability to speak and reason is the distinctive mark of our species. But much more it is our longing to become God. We do become "as" gods, but we are unable to become God. We can, at great peril, imagine being God. Or so we project. And dream.

The only way for us to fulfill our longings for God is to die. Totally surrender. Suicide is portrayed by all helping professionals as an impulse of despair, if not insanity. Or anger. Perhaps it is sometimes an expression of hunger and impatience. God is all in all, complete, lacking nothing. And so are we, except that the term of our being in flesh is accepting boundaries. So you and I are separate. Seemingly. And we can not squelch that illusion so long as we are incarnate. And thus we fight and fuck. Two seemingly opposite strategies we use to quell our separateness. I will either eliminate you or merge with you. Both promise the illusion of resolving the problem of our separateness.

Recently a piece circulated on the internet about a boy who had misbehaved in school and when he was taken to the Principal, he responded to the Principal's scolding, "Fuck you; I don't need this fucking school anyway." For which he was expelled from school.

The school sued to have him permanently expelled, and inasmuch as his family lacked funds, they were assigned a public defender. Who wrote a long, detailed, brilliant brief asking that the school's suit be dismissed. The brief, which was posted on the internet, explored the use of the term fuck, in historical and contemporary terms.

The brief began with a Google search that showed the word received more inquiries than the word Mom.

OH had a running battle with his wife about the word, which he loved and used often in conflict. (In reality so did she, being a modern woman, but she, when she acknowledged use of the word at all, insisted that it was only under his malign influence and therefore she should not be held responsible.)

He explained that the word has an emotionally satisfying double stop, the F and the K, so the word, as it emerges from one's mouth, provides for a violent blockage of air as the lips are pursed at the beginning and the throat constricts at the end.

OH heard the word everywhere, as if we have borrowed it from nature and from the modern mechanistic, chaos we call civilization.

"You listen," he suggested to his wife, "and you will hear the thumping, emotionally satisfying sound of fuck coming from every corner of your day. I do."

OH, because he was almost totally on foot as he moved about his southern California town, heard the deep, heart engaging, throbbing rap music coming from passing cars, so sturdy it seemed as if the car was powered, not by fossil fuel but by the decibels that embraced everyone and everything within a two-block radius.

After an initial period of finding it offensive and intrusive, OH learned to love it. He found it akin to the sensation of being immersed in the ocean. The medium of sound eclipsed all other sensation and wrapped itself around him. And the term most discernible, at least to OH, was fuck, his old favorite. The lowered, channeled, hot rod, or pickup raised comically onto gigantic balloon tires, rocking rhythmically to the throbbing, would cause him to alter his step so he rocked his way down the street his pace keeping time with the thumping sound coming from the truck.

It was as if the word had been created for this purpose. It punctuated the heavy throbbing sound in the most perfect, satisfying way, causing OH to wish he had been the first person ever to use the word. Creating ex-nihilo, wanting again to be God, OH was chronically subject to magical thinking, reluctant to step on a crack in the sidewalk for fear of breaking his mother's back, OH sometimes listened for fuck as he made his way to his writing station a couple of miles up the cliffs to the village, thinking that once he reached a critical mass (a million fucks?) his boundaries would melt away and he would merge with the whole of reality. Yes, he understood that was an eschatological vision, of the end of time, his time, all time.

And he found it a fucking-A thrilling vision.

Perhaps, OH thought as he walked the cliffs high above the Pacific one blustery winter day in southern California, it is time to begin thinking about heading home. Now for OH, the thought of home triggered visions of a swan-dive into the surf from the 80-foot cliff. Merging with the whole of reality was the way he saw it. Though in his best moments he recognized that his dying would alter the structure of reality hardly at all. And since it was largely his impatience, coupled with his idolatrous dream of managing the terms of his own transformation that tempted OH to dive, he disciplined himself to resist the urge.

But the vision, and the buzz it caused in him never dimmed. There are, he knows, an infinite number of ways to find one's self drawn into its place in eternity. And, whichever way we choose (or are chosen), eternity will have her way with us. Praise God.

OH Makes A Run For It

"All you ever do is bitch and talk about how lousy a job he's doing; why don't you put your money where your mouth has been all these years and run yourself?"

She startled OH. She hated being in the public eye when he was a parish priest. She couldn't be serious; she just wanted to shut him up. He knew he did complain a lot. Sort of a habit. About anyone in authority.

Matter of fact he had thought, a lot, about running for office. As an adolescent he thought he'd run for President one day, or at least the US Senate. So why not the City Council now, in his dotage?

"So I suppose you think he's doing a good job?" The two of them were into thrust and feint in the conversation now.

"Give me a break, OH. I don't particularly give a shit about the City Council. But you do. Or at least you pretend to. Couldn't get yourself elected a bishop, so why not get off your high horse and make a run for City Council. Think you've got the energy and maybe one or two good ideas."

"Look, Baby," he parried, "I've been in the death and resurrection business for 20 years. That was a hard sell to parishioners. You think I can sell that to the voters? I don't think they'll buy it."

"Neither did the people in your churches. So what else is new? Anyway, what is this death and resurrection business you like to talk about? You talk about it like you designed it. But how are you living it?"

"Fuck you," OH always wished that hadn't come out of his mouth the way it did so often, especially when she challenged him. He sometimes figured he must have a mild form of Tourette's Syndrome the way his mouth spouted off at unexpected and inappropriate moments. Though it happened almost only with her. He had promised himself he would discipline himself not to do that, but unlike his giving up drinking, sailor-mouth with his wife was a habit too ingrained and satisfying for him to wish or even discipline away.

And he knew it happened when she got too close, uncovered some reality he didn't want to face.

"OK. Sorry for the outburst. You're right on both counts. I never could sell it. And, I never have been able to live it, even though I know it's the only way. How could you ever sell surrender to a culture that worships TV? Come and get it! The big promise; everything, and everyone, including, you, dies before the new life can come. Irresistible, huh?"

"Well, there you are," she managed to say it gently, without a hint of the triumph she was feeling. "Prepared to die, run for City Council. You can go down in flames and feel more righteous and unappreciated than ever."

OH could see, even through the sarcasm dripping from her words, that she was actually on his side. She hoped he'd do it. "I would never get into a conversation with me without a layer of sarcasm to protect me," he thought.

"You know what? I just might consider doing just that. How would you like to be First Lady of the Eastover section of town?"

"Oh no you don't; don't try to foist it off on me. You want to run, you run. I've got other fish to fry. I promise not to expose you to your constituents as the erratic lech you are. If they can't discover it for themselves, they can buy you as their pig in their poke. But let me ask you this, OH, why the hell would you want to run? I mean what would you like to accomplish? What would your platform be?"

He understood that she was setting up his first debate of the campaign. She was cool, this dame. How'd he ever get lucky enough to marry her?

"First of all I'd like to run just so I could be maybe the only candidate who talks straight, doesn't worry about staying on whatever message my handlers try to foist me. Thumbing my nose at their polls would be incentive enough to get me interested."

"In what? Being assassinated? Do you understand the reason candidates are managed so carefully, even in small races like city council? It's the money, stupid. Remember Clinton having that pasted onto his eyeballs? Only he had it couched in slightly more elegant terms, as the economy. And he didn't really understand what it meant until he became our accidental candidate after Bush I imploded."

"So what did it mean? It wasn't really about the economy?"

"No, it wasn't. It meant there are some tough guys, guys you may never see or even know about, who are bank-rolling this thing, and they don't intend to see their investment go into the toilet. When money is on the line, everything else takes a back seat. Even Jack Danforth, your hero, Mr. Clean Senator and Episcopal priest told you that. If you aren't willing to play ball with the big money guys, don't bother to run."

"OH, Do you remember when Hugh Salem got himself into that construction project in Cleveland? He had done so well in Atlanta, became the biggest hottest item in the red-hot development world of Atlanta. Houses all over the world, mistress, private jet, and he figured he was ready for prime time. So he bid on a job in Cleveland, and because something sort of like Bush's campaign implosion happened in the bidding process, he won it. Then the trouble started. His shtick was delivering the job on schedule. No matter how big or complicated, he always delivered on time."

"So what's this got to do with my running for council?" OH wanted to know.

"Everything; it's about a naïve rookie bucking the big money."

"Hugh began to go nuts; everything that could go wrong on a job did. Structures collapsed, people got hurt, there were electrical fires. The job kept having to go back to restart. He got frantic, pictured not only not delivering the building on time, but losing his shirt.

"One day in the locker room at the Piedmont Shooting Club in Atlanta he was complaining to a friend, also in construction. 'Where'd you say the job was?' his friend asked.

"'Cleveland.'

"'Holy shit, Hugh, you didn't bid on a job in Cleveland? The building trades in Cleveland are all run by the mob. They control all the money in the building business in that city. Outsiders can't build there.'

"Hugh admitted that he had and that he was now mired down in a mess he didn't know how to get out of.

"And what did he do?" OH was now drawn into the story even though he didn't like connecting it to his thinking about getting into city politics.

"He went to Cleveland and met with all the guys running the job. 'Boys,' he said, hanging his head, 'I'm just a country boy from Atlanta who got lost one day and, not knowing what I was doing, landed this job in Cleveland by accident. Now I just need to get this job done and get out of here and you'll never see me in Cleveland again.'"

"What happened?" Hugh asked quietly, not wanting to hear the answer.

"The job fell into place, he delivered the building on schedule and never bid on another job anywhere in Ohio. Get it?"

"Not sure. Hope not."

"OH, you want to run for office? You'll owe your soul to the people who really run things, most of whom you not only don't know now, but you never will. Ever. Even if, by some fluke you should win. And if your candidacy should catch on, and you speak with that honest independent voice you prize, you're likely to wake up dead one morning."

"You know, you're kind of whetting my appetite."

"I figured."

OH walked outside for some fresh air. His brain was sore from the effort of trying to sort through what was happening to him.

"It switches me on to think about talking straight in a world that gave up on reality a long time ago. And bullies anyone who tries. On the other hand I have this martyr thing. I keep choosing stuff I know will hurt me."

He looked across the road to the graveyard where his parents and grandparents were buried (and several of his dogs—the city-fathers never knew about that—maybe if the word got out that he buried his dogs in the city cemetery that would be scandal enough to knock him out of a race). "Damn, I'm already looking to get dissed. I wonder if life really was simpler when those folks were above ground? Sure hope it is now."

Looking northwest always spooked OH. That was the direction their weather came from, and the sky often seemed to turn dark and ominous when he was pondering a big decision. Now, as he checked it, a huge thunder cloud, maybe 50,000 feet, looked about to swallow the earth. OH believed in signs. Sometimes.

"Darkest just before the dawn," he announced to his resting forebears. "Saddle up; we're riding into town to throw our hat in the ring."

And so he did.

That thunderstorm nearly did swallow his world before it was through with him. Whipping up hurricane-strength winds, it pelted the tin roof on their old farmhouse with a fury, like automatic gunfire. It rearranged the flower pots on the back wall, turning them into shrapnel that imbedded in the rough pine board siding that sheltered the vehicles parked in the barn. And while it did keep them from being totally destroyed, for the remainder of their tenure the red truck's windshield was pock marked and the green plastic finish on the Pathfinder turned an odd pollen yellow. Every time he tried, futilely, to wash the pollen off the truck, it reminded OH of the day he decided to forego his previously firm resolve never to enter the public arena again.

Parish pastor had nearly done him in; this would prove richer yet.

City Council, a body intended to represent people in different districts, had in fact turned out to be a way for those who wished to do business with the city to gain privileged access. Pretty much everyone understood this, though those who had not grown totally cynical still whined about the system being corrupt and unresponsive. OH knew a couple of the council members; smart. He rather liked and admired them. The youngest member struck OH as ambitious, hoping to parlay his precocious start in politics into bigger things. But the others were the sorts of old hacks one associates with city politics. People who have ingratiated themselves to many vested interests. They hope to hang on long enough to be rewarded, either with a consulting job with one of the interests, or to retire with a cool pension. Or maybe both.

As for OH, his motives were less clear, especially to himself. He knew he had hung on a few years longer than he should have in that last parish, after he had outlived his usefulness and enthusiasm for the job. He did it because he still like the cache of Rector and the perks that went with the job. And he wanted to stick around until his pension kicked in. And he still had the infernal itch, still not yet scratched.

So how was he any different? He wasn't and he knew it. His contempt wasn't for the politicians milking the system; it was for his having outgrown his own idealism.

"So that's what this is about!" OH thought. "It's my exorcism. A City Council shill just as well as a shill for Jesus. Get cleansed once and for all of my prissy self-righteousness." OH went into a reverie about the nation's presidents.

Three presidents in our era have sold themselves as bearers of whatever weird energy it is that people identify with.

Kennedy, whose father bought his Senate seat and then the White House. (Relatively inexpensively, from the Daley machine in Chicago. OH had a friend who had been a poll watcher in Chicago in 1960. He had watched old people—delivered to the polls by Democratic enforcers—vote and them go to the back of the line to vote again.) Kennedy stirred people like a rock star. In reality he was uncomfortable with nearly everyone, but he had learned to smile and greet like the Irishman he was. OH's first vote was cast for Kennedy; he never quite recovered from being wrapped in the Kennedy myth.

Ronald Reagan was a real-life movie star, but people didn't identify with him. Oddly, though Reagan was a middle class figure, he and his brittle wife were put on a pedestal by the American voter from which they never descended despite the Iran-contra scandal (in fact it was never a scandal beyond the Beltway). Even when Reagan was acknowledged as having gone gaga with Alzheimer's, he was treated as an icon, and when he died the ceremony and media adulation showed the powerful, if morbid, oddity that being dead can sometimes do more for a public figure than being alive.

But he wasn't one of us.

Now Bill Clinton, whose mother was beaten up by his drunken step-father (his biological father died in a car crash while baby Bill was preparing for gravity-existence in his mother's womb) was one of us.

He acted out a forbidden American male fantasy—unzipping his fly in a dark (but not dark enough) corner of his private office just off the Oval Office and getting a blow job from a young woman who had lifted her skirt and showed the horny young president her thong. He was one of us all right. The big difference between Clinton and Kennedy was only in part that the press had been forever changed thanks to Nixon and Watergate. The boozy good-old-boys were no longer so flattered to hang out with POTUS (as the not so Secret Service refer to the President), that they would never say or write anything to jeopardize their presidential intimacy—the big payoff of their job. Now they were a pack of serious gotchas whose ambition was to bring the president down. Clinton was the President and he had fulfilled too literally the American myth that anyone could grow up to be President. Despite being probably the smartest to hold the office, maybe ever (some say Jimmy Carter had a higher IQ), even with the Oval Office as his backdrop, he never seemed able to become larger than life. Maybe because his tough, long-suffering wife could make him grovel like any other Dagwood Bumstead, American men resented him and American women wanted to sleep with him and protect him. That was enough to get him elected twice, once against a patrician who always looked as if someone close to him had just farted, and once against a cynical war hero who too obviously never wanted the stupid job. We never worshipped Bill Clinton.

[OH, dear reader, wants you to know he loves Bill Clinton like the brother he never had. And he was envious that women flashed their thongs at him.]

And then there is George W. Bush. Whatever causes people to do that pump thing with their fist when Bush says dumb things, as if he had just scored a touchdown for their high school football team, is what OH finds repulsive. His visceral response to Bush makes OH feel lonely and pushed to the margins. He never has thought of himself as elite, but when he hears the Bush/Rove spinners speak of Bush's scorners as elite, he supposes he must be.

But there is a dimension to the GW Bush phenomenon that OH recognizes and wishes he didn't: contempt. It is written all over Bush's face whenever he faces a question he doesn't like. And, as OH learned so long ago from his therapist, one can only have contempt for one's own self. All the polls show that we don't like Bush, find him crass. But we have elected him our leader. This seemingly self-defeating dynamic leads OH to think he just might get himself elected to the City Council. He decides to teach himself to arrange his face in a look of permanent contempt.

The district in which OH lives is made up mostly of people who care very little about local politics. He has looked up the turnout in the local elections of the past decade (under 15 oercent) and he has talked with people, his neighbors after all, who tell him this. OH understands because he has never cared either. And what draws him now is a combination of ambition and boredom. Disguised terror.

He is ambitious to rise above the mediocrity of his life thus far (and the mediocrity of his neighbors) and he is bored, not merely with his own life, but with the cautious milquetoast that passes for political rhetoric.

He will take it as his task to stir up fear (and contempt) in people, just the way George W. Bush does, but instead of being about terrorism, it will be about how soon, from the perspective of geological history, each of us will be underground. And what we might want to see happen before we die. It will be a campaign based on mortality. OH will be like the bearded, white-robed guy on the corner warning about the end of time coming soon. Only instead of calling for repentance, OH will be calling for votes. Not promising that voting for him will make you immortal, or even delay your departure from the light, but simply inviting people to let go of stupid wishes to fatten their coffers when those coffers will so soon become someone else's.

Doesn't sound like a campaign designed by Karl Rove? Well, OH is no George Bush, and District 5 is hardly the White House.

"So, how about a preview of your campaign?" his long-suffering wife asked him that afternoon as the two of them were settled in the glassed-in porch for afternoon tea. They had tea every afternoon, a habit they picked up during a sabbatical year in rural Zimbabwe back in the 1980s, a couple of years after that country's bloody civil war. People OH and his wife and children visited still kept automatic weapons handy, but they never failed to stop for tea at 10:30 in the morning and 3:30 in the afternoon. OH wondered if both sides (it was not only the whites, but also the blacks who stopped for tea) might have ceased their warfare in the bush during the war at teatime. The ritual had done a lot for toning down the level of conflict between OH and his wife.

"I've thought a lot about that," OH responded, "and I think I've figured out the three main thrusts I'm going to focus on. Want to hear?"

"Have I a choice?"

OH ignored the sarcasm; he was going to have to figure out how to win the attention and support of lots harder critics than his wife if he was going to wage a campaign that had any hope of going anywhere.

"Here," he said, "are the three bulleted issues that are going to propel me into the District 5 seat on the Council. First, a resolute stand against blood doping by any athletes from our district who may be trying out for the Olympics or any other international competition."

"When, OH?" she asked, her face screwed into a knot of disgust, "has anyone from our district ever even been considered for such a thing?

"Exactly!" OH responded triumphantly. "All the other candidates will wage campaigns that look backward, that focus on issues that have already been chewed up and spit out. My campaign will anticipate what could lie ahead. Have you read the 9/11 report? What jumps out at you is that if anyone—in the CIA, in the FBI, National Security Advisor—anyone had been thinking outside the box the evidence of the impending attack was everywhere. It's just that they never considered such a possibility. So John Ashcroft told George Tenant to fuck off, stop bothering him about things that were so remote.

"No, we never have had anyone from our district compete in the Olympics. And no one had ever flown a plane into the Twin Trade Towers either. Thanks to my campaign, my forward looking vigilance, we're going to be ready when the first person comes along."

"Brilliant!" OH wasn't sure whether she was being sarcastic or serious, but he was on a roll. He felt his blood pressure mounting.

"Second issue is preventing Brazil from developing a nuclear capability."

"Oh, good, OH, we sure wouldn't want that, not here in District 5."

"I didn't expect you to think this was a real issue, but hear me out. You may be unaware that for several years Brazil has been getting material from Pakistan, enough to build a nuclear capacity. They may be within a couple of years of being able to build a bomb."

"Brazil? And how does this impact District 5?"

"Yep, Brazil. Sick of being patronized by the U.S., they are looking to challenge our hegemony in the region, force us to redraw the Monroe Doctrine. Have you heard anything about this from Washington? No. From NPR which is supposed to be our unbiased source of news? No.

"You'll hear it first from me in my campaign for the District 5 seat. It will be a wake up call for the whole nation, begun right here."

"But what's going to make the people of our district, who are mostly concerned with unleashed dogs shitting on their lawns, and pot holes, give a damn about Brazil's nuclear potential?"

"You sound just like the people who surrounded Al Gore and John Kerry in the last two presidential elections. They looked over the shoulder of the people who had run Bush's campaign and copied what they saw. And lost."

"But Bush won."

"Of course, because his handlers had him sounding as if he was interested in doing something others hadn't been brave enough to try, and because he made big complicated issues sound like ordinary stuff, stuff anyone could understand. He actually didn't have any better issues; just talked about them in a way that seemed accessible to ordinary people."

"And how is it that you're going to make nuclear non-proliferation for Brazil sound like an accessible concern for those of us who live in this backwater?"

"Do you remember the last time Ashcroft raised our alert level? Well, I don't know if you were aware of it, but that had a dramatic impact on our budget right here in District 5."

"Give me a break, OH."

"Truly. We had all our school buses retrofitted with alert radios so the drivers could know immediately if there was an emergency. That cost us almost $100,000."

"How the hell do you know that? I've never heard a word about it."

"Well you're going to when my campaign gets going. It's a disgrace that neither my opponent nor anyone else has paid any attention to it. And do you feel safer because of it? That hundred-thousand dollars could have been used to clean up that men's toilet in the park where homeless people hang out and do drugs and sex."

"You sound ready to do battle, OH. I assume you've got the data on this so you can substantiate it."

"Did you ever see any evidence from the guys who claimed Kerry really hadn't earned those battle decorations? I don't think so. They just called press conferences and made a lot of accusations with indignant sounding voices and Fox news took care of the rest. Not to mention Saddam Hussein and weapons of mass destruction. We sure punished Bush at the polls for not having any evidence for that, didn't we?"

"You're shitting me, OH. You mean you're creating this stuff out of whole cloth and then bandying it around as if it were true, knowing the media will do your heavy lifting? That's repulsive, beyond gross."

"Hey, wait a minute; do you think it's a good idea that Brazil become a nuclear power? So long as there is a nuclear threat within our own hemisphere we're going to have to spend an inordinate part of our resources to protect ourselves. This is a local issue, and a big one."

"You know what I mean, OH. The $100,000 for the school buses to get radios; did you make that up or did it really happen?"

"Look, you're just like every other loser; you lack imagination. If we wait for shit to happen, we'll be behind the eight ball forever. What this district needs is a visionary, someone who can see what's on the horizon."

"Maybe you should run for attorney general."

"It's more important for me to run here, where these things can be nipped in the bud. By the time it gets to the national level, the layers of bureaucracy have gotten so thick, and the self-interest so intense that action has become almost impossible. You want to see action, talk to parents about their children and the buses that take them to school every morning and bring them home every afternoon."

"You'll be the only candidate in the county, for sure, who has athletes' doping and no nukes for Brazil at the heart of his campaign."

"Precisely. The others will be talking about potholes. Who's going to sound like the statesman we all want leading our country."

"We're talking county, not country, OH."

"You watch. And I've got one more big issue. Arlen Specter."

"Arlen Specter? The Senator from Pennsylvania? We don't even live in Pennsylvania, OH. What's Arlen Specter got to do with District 5?"

"You know he chairs the Senate Judiciary Committee, right? And did you know that some of the right-wing crazies from his own party are trying to dislodge him from that chair so they can get Bush's conservative judges' nominations onto the floor?"

"Yeah, I've read some about that. And how does that fit into the race for the City Council seat for District 5?"

"Think about it. We've got two hospitals and a birthing center right here in old District 5. How many people do they employ? More than any other business in the District. How many abortions do you suppose they do a year? And how many women, women who check you out at the super market and clean your house or work in the insurance agency that insures your car, have had to have abortions in the past five years?"

"I have no clue."

"Exactly. And thanks to the Patients Bill of Rights—another target of the right-wingers in Washington, neither does anyone else. This is the stealth bomber of this campaign, an issue that looks distant, so remote from us as to not matter. And if no one raises it, the damage will be done before anyone even knows it matters."

"OH, I've got to hand it to you, or maybe distance myself from you; you sound like you've conceived a campaign modeled on the shit we have seen from the right wing for the past two decades. Think up stuff that stirs up the anxieties in people, whether it has any substance or not, accuse the other side of neglecting or exacerbating the issue, even with no evidence, and voila! You've given the media a reason to give you space."

"Hey, you want to win or you want to be pure?"

Even as he explained all this, OH understood his issues, compelling as they were (even though he planned perfect his presentation so voters would indignantly spout concerns they never knew they had), were in fact smoke and mirrors. In the same way that George Bush, though he had grooved his talk about terrorism, the Iraq War, unemployment and tax relief, was, OH knew, only ever delivering a single message:

I am one of you and he isn't.

It didn't particularly matter that the candidate was John Kerry and not cherry-cheeked John Edwards. (Though Kerry, with his snow boarding and $5K bicycle fit the bill better than any other potential rival.) It was about stirring our contempt for the other guy, our fear of him. OH knew that Bush had cultivated his back-country Texas drawl through years of coaching. His brother Jeb, who grew up in the same house and town, when he became Governor of Florida, a southern/northern state, and who was on TV constantly during the hurricane assault in the fall of 2004, had a flat nasal Greenwich, Connecticut accent without a trace of the Texas his brother had. (OH wondered that no one in the media ever mentioned it. He couldn't have been the only one who noticed. Of course he wasn't dependent on the largesse of the President of the Unites States as the media were.)

"I've got a subliminal message that is even more powerful than Bush's I am-one-of-you-and-he-isn't," OH said to his still disbelieving wife. Or was it that she didn't wish to be implicated?

"And what might that be?"

"Listen to this; mind you there is a slightly different twist to the message for men and for women. It has to be delivered in the same way, but so that it will impact you Venus dwellers in a different, almost reverse way from how it hits us Mars guys.

"For the men: that woman you have been dreaming about, who will not only love and fuck you without ceasing, but who will care for you without the tension and resentment that is messing up your life, is out there waiting for you. It's because of the screwed-up way our society has arranged us that there has been a disconnect on this. You deserve that dream woman and you can have her. And all you have to do is vote for me, join our effort, and things will begin to fall your way."

"And for the women?" She laughed. She hadn't meant to; it snuck out unexpectedly. She thought what he was saying was gross, beyond politically incorrect. But she found herself enjoying it, getting into it.

"That's the easy part for me," OH said, "because I am a bona fide man wired up much like a woman. Here's the message for women:

"The bullshit you have been putting up with can stop. The posturing, having to tip toe around that guy so he doesn't take offense, the stroking and faking sexual excitement, and all the other countless ways you have to stroke his fragile ego so he won't interfere with your running the show, your needing to disguise your contempt for his incompetence and adolescent wish to be seen as a world beater—all that can be let go of if you will simply let me have your vote."

"Even if you are, as you say, wired up like a woman, when women look at you they see a guy. How are you going to get them to do what no woman in her right mind would do, which is trust and believe that you are any different from all the other men in the world who will say or do anything to get into a woman's pants? Or get their vote?"

"There! You've just revealed the big secret of my campaign. Reassure women that men will do anything to get into their drawers, and that, being male, I understand, and that being wired differently, I also know how to exploit that without triggering the violent response women fear from men when the men understand they have lost control. When men realize they've lost the war. Become dangerous."

"The whole thing is about control; who has it and who will relinquish it. Ever notice Bush's appointments and how they meld into and, at the same time, reverse the macho dynamic of his message? He takes an attractive, but manageably attractive, woman of-color to be his war advisor. He went Clinton one better than Clinton's appointment of Madelyn Albright as his secretary of state. The problem with Albright was she was too scary for men to imagine fucking. They thought she must have Clinton's balls in her pocket book.

"Now Condi Rice, there's a chick everyone would like to cuddle with, and the women get it that she has power while the men imagine that Bush has access to her like Clinton had with Monica Lewinsky."

"Fascinating. And how do you translate it into no blood-doping for athletes, no nukes for Brazil, and the judiciary chair for Arlen Specter?"

"Think about it; it's built in. The blood doping for men is about giving them equal opportunity to stardom, while for women it is about keeping the lid on the testosterone that threatens to undo the human experiment on this planet. Every man believes that if he can star at something, anything, he will gain access to the wonder-woman who will promote his DNA into the next generation. But he thinks the deck is stacked against him. I promise to unstack the deck, giving him back his hope."

"And women know they can out-think men. Their fear is that male aggression will trump their superior intellect. Opposing blood doping sends the message that this candidate is going to put a stop (albeit unwittingly since I'm a guy) to the effort to ratchet up male chemistry."

"The no nukes for Brazil is a no-brainer. It has the color and the gender thing. The men, even men of color in this country, fear any threat to our hegemony, particularly from anyone in our hemisphere, particularly of another race. Brazil is perhaps the most racially heterodox country on earth. The Monroe Doctrine is about a lot more than just commerce. We own this hemisphere and we intend to keep it. Brazil? Give me a break. You think American manhood is going to stand by and watch while Brazil makes a run at us? I don't think so."

"Not only that; you've seen the pictures of those women in their Brazilian bikinis. If we subdue their men, we could have a shot at their women."

"For women it's about macho Brazilian men, who still behave as though keeping women pregnant and barefoot is sensible, all the while having their finger on the nuclear button. Since the beginning of time the only threat to female domination of the world has been male attraction to combat, which is compensation for our inferior role in making babies. If we can't reproduce we can destroy. What you make we can unmake. And give us powerful enough toys to play with and we will."

"Thus, no nukes for Brazil."

"Brilliant, huh?"

"As for Arlen Specter and the Judiciary Committee, it's got it all. Specter has already shown himself to be a groveler. When the assassains in the Republican Party went after him for saying the what everybody knew. He said that any appointee who said he would vote to undo Row vs. Wade would never get out of the Judiciary Committee. The Republican enforcers said he had failed the basic litmus test. And he caved. Big time."

"The fight is only peripherally about abortion rights. The real battle is about power and control. Specter showed himself to be obedient to the posturing men who want to regain the public face of male domination even while they fear women and understand women will never let it happen. At the same time women have believed that Specter is going to protect their interests when the shooting starts."

"Arlen Specter," she protested, not bothering to hide her disgust, "is a candy-ass and no self-respecting woman would let him get in charge of our interests." It pleased OH to see that she was not only understanding his campaign, but beginning to really get into it.

"Yes and no. Yes, he is a candy ass. Like all males, right? But, while it's true that women wouldn't let him take charge of their interests, they would let him, and all of us males, enjoy the illusion of control so long as we were in fact doing your bidding. Which describes Arlen Specter's career as a senator, and certainly his role as chair of the Senate Judiciary Committee."

"OK, OH, now, tell me what you really think about this stuff yourself. Not what you think will play to the voters, but what you think. Because unless you at least go through the process in a serious way, internalizing the message, figuring what's real for you and what's bull shit, I don't care how clever your campaign is, you're going to end up like Al Gore and John Kerry. Know what I'm saying?"

"I've thought a lot about that and I'm going to tell you what I won't say to anyone else, and will deny if you tell anyone else. I am embedded in this culture the way those combat reporters are embedded with the American troops in Iraq. You know it's not that the combat journalists have lost their integrity and are reporting only our propaganda. They're getting shot at just like the guys they're writing about. They understand in a way you and I can't why those seemingly nice middle-American kids fucked with those Iraqi prisoners so cruelly."

"I'm a white male with a primitive survival drive, powerfully formed at an early age by this culture. I'm pretty damn smart about parsing it, figuring out what's up with it, but not so swift at stepping back and seeing how it works on me."

"OH, are you telling me that you don't know what of your brilliant platform is clever manipulation and what is your personal conviction?"

"That's what I'm saying, and what's more, I don't think that makes me any different from almost everyone who ever runs for office, and I would include Gore and Kerry in that. I always wondered, especially with a seeming knuckle-head like George Bush how much of him is a pose and how much real. Now that I've put myself in a position similar to his, however much lower on the food-chain, I get it in a very discomforting way. I no longer think his seeming stupidity is a pose, even though I suspect he's a really smart guy."

"And how's that work? He appears stupid but he's smart, and he's not faking?"

"Look, he's likely got some sort of learning-disability issue that causes him to measure himself unfavorably against his patrician father. So, right from the start, he played this role of the tough cowboy. It released him from the expectations that he would follow his father's preppy straight path. Sure, he went to Andover and Yale, Harvard Business School. But have a look at what people thought of him in those places, which, by the way, were opened to him because of his family connections. I bet he'd have given his left nut to be left alone to drink and be a roughneck in the Texas oil field."

"So what is he? An American. Seemingly slow-witted but tough and pragmatic. Take no shit."

"Christ, if I keep this up I'm going to talk myself into loving the guy. And I really hate him."

"You mean you hate the part of him that seduces you into wanting to be like him."

"Precisely. I don't think it's good for the country to have a guy working out his issues with his father while he's running the country. But anyone who gets anywhere near that office will be working out his issues, with his father, with his mother, with his dog and with God, for Christ's sakes. It's just the way the human psyche works."

"Hmmm. Bush had a big drinking problem, right? You, too, right?"

"Yep. And you know how his turned around? His wife put the wood to him, told him she was going to leave him unless he did something about his drinking."

"Get it? The voters got it. He was a male American fool, a drunk, because he felt like tits on a bull, useless. Until his wife intervened. Most people would think he changed because she threatened him. In fact the message was that she thought he was competent, not incompetent, and that was the first time in his life anyone whose opinion of him mattered. She was the first person who got close enough so he thought she had taken him seriously. The strongest incentive for his becoming a sober born again was believing he could. She didn't just threaten or bully him; she believed in him."

"And how do you know all this."

"The way we all know anything; intuition, projection and imagination. I've been there. And even more than questions about parking or taxes, nukes or doping, that complicated dynamic is what I want to run on, why I'm going to run."

"You know, OH, I can imagine a lot worse motives, but I wonder if running for office is really what you want to do. Take a look at any of the people who have run for whatever office. Do they seem like evolved productive people to you? They don't to me. My sense is that they are still trying to work out those disappointments they think their parents and their mentors feel about them. Maybe that's what's up for you, too. But if it's about your vocation, what your soul is calling you to, I don't know."

OH suddenly was exhausted, drained, felt like he had run a marathon. He sighed from some place so deep inside that it startled him, as if some archaeological remnant, buried in his marrow millions of years ago, had been unearthed.

"Maybe this is what George Bush felt like," he thought, "when Laura confronted him about his drinking.

"My soul? OH protested, "Who knows about one's soul and what it's calling to us?"

"Sometimes I think you do. It's what first drew me to you; it's what makes me often want to make a wide turn around you. I listen to you talk about that bullshit that stands for serious political stuff, and you turn it into something so real and compelling that I almost want to get involved with politics myself. Then I pick up a paper and see how it gets treated. You understand; it's throwing your pearls before swine. Now you know why Jesus said not to do that."

"Fuck Jesus!"

"I know, sweetheart." She hadn't referred to OH as sweetheart since the days when sex trumped everything else in their life. "The miserable prick won't leave you alone, will he? Of course it's pretty reciprocal; you keep bugging Jesus, too, as if he had something powerful in mind for you."

"Ever try to unpack 'Render under Caesar . . . '?"

"Give me a break." he complained.

"Why should I? You'd hate me if I did."

And OH knew that she was right. Even while he longed for her to reassure him, to tell him he was better than he knew he was, on the rare occasions when she had, he waved her off, held her in contempt for coddling him.

He didn't make the race.

It was not only because he ran out of steam before he collected the required 250 people to sign his nominating petition. He also knew that he had accomplished what he hoped, struggling in his conversations with his wife, and even more in his conversations with himself, to find the way between his passion for setting things right and the insight into himself he had gained through long and painful inner work. He began to see the campaign as another of his futile attempts to justify his existence.

"And no wonder," he said to himself, "that so few people wanted to sign my petition. They knew instinctively what I had not yet faced. I was trying to get them to write legislation for my life rather than the reverse. I was trying to get them to finish my life-journey for me."

OH understood that Tip O'Neil (who now, free from gravity and O_2 dependence, no doubt understood his own wisdom better than when he offered it) was so right when he said that all politics is local. Only he meant Honey Fitz' old silk-stocking/working-class Irish district in Boston. OH has come to understand his insight as meaning local as in his own inner self.

It was the day OH was finishing off a meeting with the woman he had chosen to be his campaign manager, as he was confessing to her that he had chosen her the same way he had identified his three campaign issues; to distract himself and them. The afternoon he told her about watching whales fuck, she said she knew he wasn't going to end up making the race. She saw his other agenda was going to eclipse any run for the District 5 seat. OH felt the ecstasy course through him, endorphins bathing his every cell.

OH thought he felt his body lighten, as if it was freeing itself of the earth's gravity. His brain flooded with blood, releasing endorphins, giving him a sense of ecstasy much like the feeling he remembered that day in his kayak, "I feel as if I could make love to you or maybe to the whole world right now."

She laughed, "You'd need an apparatus like the whales, huh?"

And there is that leviathan.

EPILOGUE

OH would always wonder about his vocation as priest, especially as parish priest. He felt a priest to the end. In his marrow. But leader of a parish had come to feel more and more restrictive, about minding an institution. Minding a parochial, political agenda.

One November day, several years after he had laid down his parish mantle, he went to the dentist, a young dentist who had come to his last parish shortly before OH retired to wonder. The young dentist told him this was clergy day in his practice. OH's successor, in almost every respect his mirror opposite, was coming in immediately after him. His successor had a tumultuous tenure, marked by conflict with parishioners (a different group from those with whom OH had battled) who regarded his 90s Texas fast-lane life offensive and lacking piety. OH rather admired the man's defying of the conventional projections of parishioners who were uneasy about their own appetites.

So they passed—these two instruments, tools of God's ineffable machinations in the late 20th and early 21st centuries—cautiously, trying not to arouse the unresolved issues stirring in each other's dim unconscious. Eager to let lie the ghosts they consciously dismissed, but that walked just behind them everywhere, nipping at their heels.

OH got his parking ticket stamped by the receptionist and descended to the bowels of the building. Parked in the two spots reserved for patients was OH's 12-year-old Volvo station wagon, the vehicle-of-choice for surfers and refugees from the 60s. And in the other spot his successor's brand-spanking-new gray Porsche Boxster.

OH smiled, backing cautiously from his space, so as not to scratch his colleague's Porsche.

A dignified, aging Volvo and an in-your-face Porsche, toasting the schizophrenia through which the culture was wandering. Two designated holy-men, initiates from an ancient guild precariously bridging the chasm that has marked every guild, sacred and secular, since we humans started trying to sort out our differences. As he backed slowly out of his parking space, admiring the Porsche and his successor's bravado in driving it, OH felt grateful that he would never, not in this life, know what lay at the bottom of that chasm. Or if the chasm had a bottom. Or was a chasm.

OH rode his modest mount back to his simple writing station, his carrel in the library at the Museum of Contemporary Art. After his morning designer-coffee he needed a trip to the loo. His usual tucked-away men's room was occupied so he detoured to the bathroom in the public part of the building. As he opened the door of the stall to the toilet he was struck by an image.

The stall reminded him of photos he had seen of the sterile room (he assumed it was sterile, though the notion was disorienting) in a prison death-house, a hospital-type cubicle reserved for executions by lethal injection. The plain tile walls, the metal door. This up-to-date men's room had a pull-down table on which a modern father may change his baby's diaper. The table was reminiscent of the gurney on which they strap the doomed person and swab his arm so he will not get an infection in the ensuing seconds before they stream eternity into him.

As he released some of his body's surplus fluids into the toilet, OH wondered how long . . .

So it goes.

Death be not proud.

Printed in the United States
40761LVS00001B/3

9 781413 495058